For the Good of the World

Other books by the same author

ACADEMIC
An Introduction to Philosophical Logic
The Refutation of Scepticism
Berkeley: The Central Arguments
Wittgenstein
Russell
Philosophy 1: A Guide through the Subject (editor)
Philosophy 2: Further through the Subject (editor)
The Continuum Encyclopedia of British Philosophy (editor)
Truth, Meaning and Realism
Scepticism and the Possibility of Knowledge
The History of Philosophy

GENERAL
The Long March to the Fourth of June (with Xu You Yu, as Li Xiao Jun)
China: A Literary Companion (with Susan Whitfield)
The Future of Moral Values
The Quarrel of the Age: The Life and Times of William Hazlitt
Herrick: Lyrics of Love and Desire (editor)
Five Poems
What Is Good?
Descartes: The Life and Times of a Genius
Among the Dead Cities
Against All Gods
Towards the Light
The Choice of Hercules
Ideas that Matter
To Set Prometheus Free
Liberty in the Age of Terror
The Good Book
The God Argument
A Handbook of Humanism (editor, with Andrew Copson)
Friendship
The Age of Genius
War
Democracy and Its Crisis
The Good State
The Frontiers of Knowledge

ESSAY COLLECTIONS
The Meaning of Things
The Reason of Things
The Mystery of Things
The Heart of Things
The Form of Things
Thinking of Answers
The Challenge of Things

For the Good of the World

*Is Global Agreement on
Global Challenges Possible?*

A. C.
GRAYLING

A Oneworld Book

First published by Oneworld Publications, 2022

ISBN 978-0-86154-266-6
eISBN 978-0-86154-267-3

Typeset by Hewer Text UK Ltd
Printed and bound in Great Britain by Clays Ltd, Elcograf S.p.A.

Oneworld Publications
10 Bloomsbury Street
London WC1B 3SR
England

The rivers of time flow down through the
daughters of my house and their daughters.
They make the good of the world and pass it on,
because they remember the future.
For Georgie, Maddie and Eva with love.

CONTENTS

INTRODUCTION

Can we humans agree on a set of values which will allow us to confront the numerous threats that we and our planet face – *we* collectively, given that there are no exceptions for any one group of people or nation from the problems in question?

Or will we continue our disagreements, rivalries, and antipathies, even as we collectively approach what, in the not impossible extreme, might be drastic global threats even to the risk of extinction?

If there is a set of values we can agree on, a universal ethical outlook that can guide us away from the consequences of our historical choices and activities, what is it? How are we to begin overcoming the diversity of attitudes across cultures about – for chief examples – the sources and uses of social and political authority, economic imperatives, justice, religion, discrimination and prejudice, the position of women in society, sex and sexuality, science, evolution, the entangled and often painful legacies of history, and how to deal with the challenge of climate change? Is it hopelessly utopian to work for an end to division, conflict, and disagreement, and instead for all humanity to find common ground to solve the problems faced by our planet and its peoples?

The problem of *relativism* in ethics – 'what I think is good you think is bad' with no apparent way of resolving the contradiction – has long been a familiar one. In the safe realm of theory one solution to it is to 'live and let live', accepting irreconcilability. But in the realm of practice, in our inescapably globalized world, that is a luxury which cannot be indulged, because where outlooks collide the result is too often and too literally disastrous, as acts of terrorism and interethnic and interreligious conflicts show.

The phrase used in the previous sentence, 'our inescapably globalized world', captures a major part of the problem humanity faces.

Globalization – a word so over-worked that every use of it looks like a cliché – has a long history. Its modern form began in the fifteenth century CE when Portugal's Prince Henry the Navigator encouraged his country's sailors to explore, a process that evolved into seeking sea routes to sources of the East's desirable products, especially spices. Until then these valuable commodities had been transported to Arabia's shores and laboriously conveyed to the Mediterranean coast by camel. By the end of the sixteenth century, following the lead of Portugal's seamen, European commercial navies sailing across the equator and round the Cape of Good Hope had effectively made that route redundant. Very soon afterwards they began transporting human cargo – slaves – westward to the New World, bringing back gold and silver, and later sugar, cotton, and tobacco.

As globalization increased almost exclusively in the form of trade and colonization it disseminated Europe's ideas, faiths, and ways of life across the planet, changing much in the societies encountered. The process was partial and gradual as long as communications were constrained by distance. Full globalization became imminent when rapid and reliable international communications by rail, telegraph, and mail became common-place, and reached its recent apogee with universal air travel and the internet.

Globalization will only stall or go into reverse if a major planetary catastrophe occurs that disrupts the millions of bonds that have come to wrap the planet round. One possible cause would be pandemic disease, which might diminish globalization's physical manifestations until means of controlling it are found; the Covid-19 pandemic is a stark warning of what the future may hold. Another is the fact that the internet has turned out to be a platform for so much harmful content, which could result in censorship and control being imposed, diminishing the electronic version of globalization too. Because the world's interconnectedness is a key to the world's economy, with few places left that can hope to flourish without the lifelines to other places and people along which economic and cultural exchanges flow, the retreat of globalization will have negative effects along with positive ones. For example, it will reverse the slow and unequal trend towards reducing world poverty, and could exacerbate the problems of inequality and economic injustice that have been major factors in the rise of right-wing populism in the early decades of the twenty-first century.

As the Covid-19 pandemic showed, the planet's degree of interconnectedness is a risk as well as a benefit. Pandemics aside, interconnectedness promotes economic competition as well as mutual dependency, and because economic success depends on growth and profits, which in turn depend on controlling costs and promoting consumption, the strains on the physical and social fabric of the planet increase. So even in good times, more intensive techniques of production, more technological innovation, more movements of people, bring problems, and too often threats, as well as increases in wealth and knowledge.

The threats include anthropogenic – human-caused – climate change, epidemic diseases, malign or harmful uses of technology such as spyware and autonomous weapons systems, competition turning into conflict, and violent reactions by groups whose traditional values are threatened by various forms of modernization. Globalization also raises acute questions about human rights and social and economic justice, given the pressures it exerts in the relentless quest for cheap labour, new markets and natural resources, with consequent enforced juxtaposition of competing or mutually hostile value outlooks. Conflicts force refugees across borders, economic disparities promote migration, with people being both pushed and pulled: pushed by deprivation or conflict at home and pulled by the attraction of wealth and peace elsewhere – an age-old dynamic, but problematic in a more crowded planet.

As the world globalizes and the rate of technological change increases, more conservative outlooks – not least those involving religion and nationalism – work to resist their influence, increasing conflict. The concepts of race, sex, gender, sexuality, educational value, and biology are all foci of difficulty and contestation therefore.

Almost all the problems are not such that they can be solved or even managed within the borders of a single state. Globalization really does mean *globalization*. By far the most obvious example is anthropogenic climate change. Only a concerted global effort can stop the rise in the planet's temperatures to levels where many species are tipped into extinction and much of humanity itself is endangered. But global efforts are also needed to deal with pandemic diseases; global agreement is needed to control the development of potentially dangerous technologies, especially weapons technologies; global agreement is needed to solve the problems that cause conflicts, mass migrations, violence, and risks to both national and international stability.

And here therefore is the problem at issue: there is no worldwide set of values that can be invoked to underwrite agreements about what to do and not do in the interests of humanity and the planet in all these respects. This question, therefore – *Is a system of universally acceptable values possible?* – counts as one of the most important that humankind can ask itself, in the hope of achieving a positive answer.

It turns out, on examination, that these different problems do have a single solution, which is not obvious until the explanation for it shows why it is right, at which point, paradoxically, it becomes obvious. To understand this, and more particularly to understand how it can be made to work to humanity's advantage, we need to see why globalized agreement is necessary to deal with each of the problems. In this book I seek to do this by focusing on the three most pressing challenges that face the world: climate change, troubling aspects of technological development, and deficits of social, economic, and political justice.

The first problem, global warming, is or by now should be familiar. It is possibly the most tractable problem faced by the world among those mentioned, because ways of reducing the rate of warming, mitigating its effects, and adapting to some of its consequences, are known and within reach – provided that humanity as a whole works together, and in such a way as to share the costs and burdens of doing so. The required action bears on production and consumption – which means: on economic activity; therefore, on economies. On the face of it, a straightforward reduction in production and consumption seems to imply a reduction in living standards and quality of life for all, but most markedly in the wealthier countries of the world. This is what has made the political parties who form governments in these countries reluctant to take the kind or at least the degree of action necessary. But the solutions do not have to necessitate a drop in living standards, and indeed had better not involve them, given that raising populations out of poverty itself implies increases in the production and consumption on which living standards depend. Therefore the means and methods of production, and what is consumed, have to be the targets of climate change action: wholesale use of clean renewable energy sources is a key target, sustainable development the imperative. The chief barrier to achieving the goal of keeping the rise in average global temperature to below 2° Celsius is the application of what will be described shortly as the negative corollary of what, as the coiner of it, I have elsewhere called 'Grayling's Law', described later.

The second problem, technology, which in its beneficial aspects is a great boon to humanity – and most of its aspects are indeed beneficial – contains within it the potential to be a source of danger to individuals and society. This appears most acutely in the form of some potential uses of AI (artificial intelligence) – not least, but not exclusively, in weapon systems, already in development. There is much misunderstanding about the kinds of risks that technology can pose; much of the anxiety about AI is misplaced and based on instinctive reactions to what is merely unfamiliar. But the real risks are great, ranging from threats to individual privacy through the undermining of democratic institutions and government to the unleashing of unpredictable escalations in conflicts. Humanity-wide agreement is necessary to guard against misdirection and misuse in technological development, because without it national imperatives against falling behind in technological arms-races will be irresistible.

But there are other, currently less visible, technological developments that will raise acute ethical questions: for a prime example, medical technologies. Advances in neuroscience already offer the possibility of brain-monitoring 'lie detector' capabilities; enhanced surgical and medical control of emotion, behaviour, and memory; invasion of privacy by recording the content of neural circuit activation; and more. Advances in genetic engineering and stem cell research offer the possibility of modifying and enhancing human beings from womb to old age. Such enhancement will be more available to the rich than the poor; a *Brave New World*-type diversification in the human lineage could inevitably result. Conquering the deficits of ageing raises questions about very long-lived and healthy populations and their economic and social impact, the latter illustrated by such questions as – for just one example – what social decisions will be required if women can continue to have babies when aged 80 or 100, and choose to do so: will having offspring have to be rationed?

The third problem, justice and rights, on the face of it looks like a miscellany: homosexuality, and sexuality in general; gender inequality; faith and secularity; the lingering effects of historical wrongs such as genocides and slavery; law, rights, and liberty; economic justice. But there are themes that connect all these disparate-seeming topics, and addressing them is crucial to global peace, because each of them is a familiar and frequent trigger for discord. Of the three problems, this seems at once the least urgent and most intractable, and perhaps for that reason it is relatively neglected in thinking about how to manage the world's problems. But in fact it is the divisions and oppositions in this category that underlie the inability to reach a world-united front in dealing properly with the other problems. This is because these divisions underlie the reluctance to be left behind in economic and military competitions, and as a result obstruct international cooperation. It is to this category of justice that efforts to achieve the UN's Sustainable Development Goals belong; these goals are fundamentally about justice for everyone in humankind, and their achievement requires overcoming the sources of division at issue.

The sources of division and difficulty in the world have two principal roots. One is a law of action which, as mentioned earlier, I call 'Grayling's Law':

> *Anything that CAN be done WILL be done if it brings advantage or profit to those who can do it.*

This means that development of autonomous weapons systems, genetic engineering of foetuses, technologies that reduce civil liberties, *will* be developed, whether by public or private agencies seeing the utility and profit in doing so, or that dare not risk being left behind in the arms race of technological innovation. They *will* happen therefore, despite every effort to prevent or outlaw them.

And there is a corollary, every bit as negative, which is:

> *What CAN be done will NOT be done if it brings costs, economic or otherwise, to those who can stop it*

– such as controlling climate change caused by human activity, eradicating tropical diseases in poor regions of the world, introducing systems of democracy and civil liberties that deny concentration of power in the hands of partisan economic or ideological interests.

In effect, this double-edged Law is a law of self-interest. Self-interest is rational when proportional to other concerns, and governed by principle; when it is short-term and knows that others might be harmed by it, it has other names – in descending order of acceptability: self-interest, short-termism, selfishness, callousness, greed.

The second root of the world's difficulties is ideology: political, social, moral, and religious ideologies, commitments to ways of thinking and acting that govern whole populations, or influential groups within them, in ways that can be distorting and limiting, even dangerous. The historical sources of division lie in conflicts of ideology as much as, if not indeed more than, in competition for wealth and power. Often enough, these sources of division exist in service to one another.

If there is to be a chance of finding ways to generate universal agreement on how global problems can be confronted – at least managed, if not solved – the underlying question of values has to be addressed. This is the hard part, all the harder for being confronted by the massive challenge of what is implied in the two parts of the self-interest 'Law' and the fundamental ideological differences that separate states and cultures. The solution to global problems has to be sought here. But even in the most conciliatory spirit of seeking compromises that might allow a global solution to the globe's problems, there are certain sticking-points which add to the difficulty. Here a challenge to make tough choices about what is *right* cannot be dodged, and a principled case for them has to be made, in the hope of persuading those whose traditions and beliefs make them unwilling to accept, or perhaps in their own view incapable of accepting, that case.

This means that the problems themselves have to be properly understood. Generalizations about climate change, inequality, and technology are insufficient for identifying where the value-questions really bite. Accordingly, I examine what is at stake in each of the areas of challenge so that questions of these essential kinds can be answered: 'What is really at stake here? What do we most care about as regards what might happen, and what might we have to do or cease doing to stop that happening? What do we need in the way of assurance that our fear of X will not be realized if we do the Y that seems to be necessary to prevent/promote Z?'

Either humanity makes some choices and accepts the challenge of living them out, or the choices will be made for us by circumstances, too late for us to have any say in the matter. That is the simple, inescapable, and dangerous reality that faces us now.

A final thought: it is not impossible that the saddest sentiment expressible in any language – 'it's too late' – is already true. These pages might be written in an aftermath already here but as yet unrecognized. One can think of many examples in history of irreversible change having happened before anyone understood that it had happened, let alone before the passing of opportunities to prevent or mitigate its consequences, or guide them in more positive directions. Yet to act as if one thinks so is defeatist. One must strive to the last moment and the last ounce of strength, mindful of those who, all too probably, will inherit from us increased burdens with diminished resources because of what we and those who came before us have done.

1

CONFRONTING THE DANGER
OF A WARMING WORLD

Global warming is happening, its effects are already being felt, the harm to humanity, other species, and the planet is increasing, and too much of it is already irreversible. The *further* dangers that threaten if the global temperature rises above 2° Celsius are devastating – and if the all too real possibility of an increase to 4° Celsius happens by 2100, the result will be that many of today's children will be faced with a literally catastrophic situation, with hundreds of millions of starving and desperate refugees fleeing from extensive regions of our planet made uninhabitable by floods, droughts, pestilence, storms, and fire, and therefore with conflict escalating as settled populations, themselves already struggling with economic and social difficulties, contend with migrant populations numbering in the millions and tens of millions, entering their territory in a frantic quest for food and shelter.

This apocalyptic vision is not fiction. It is, in sober fact, a real possibility. The world is facing an extreme emergency. Its governments and far too many of its people are behaving as if they are blind to this fact, despite the increasingly frightened chorus of concern from science and climate groups, despite the careful and detailed analyses regularly published by the UN's International Panel on Climate Change (IPCC), and despite the periodic international summits at which governments agree to act, but which so far have had woefully insufficient effect – as illustrated by the fact that in the decade following the Kyoto Protocol's adoption in 1997 global greenhouse gas emissions rose faster than in the decade preceding it.[1]

In order to focus minds, discussion of the dramatic warming trend in the planet's climate should concentrate on *potential worst-case* scenarios, that is, on the far too great possibility that it will cause *severe* harm to humanity along with other species and the environment generally. Focusing on the potential worst-case harms identifies the efforts required to prevent them happening, or at least to mitigate them or to prepare to adapt wherever mitigation is unfeasible. 'Should' implies that even if it is not *certain* that the most harmful effects will occur – if it is 'merely' *possible* that they might occur – the risks are so great that efforts to prevent or mitigate them, or at least to prepare to adapt, are essential.

This is the rational strategy. It is not rational merely to hope that warming will be restrained. It is not rational to bank on the chance of less severe outcomes. The evidence is that humanity's efforts to moderate climate warming are, so far, very unpromising. Competition, rivalry, ignorance both genuine and wilful, and the malign effects of the self-interest Law are all already and in fact actively against the survival of humanity and the planet. To put matters bluntly: collective suicide is currently and actually in progress; the intervention required to prevent or moderate it is beyond urgent.

It should by now be common knowledge that average global temperatures have risen markedly since the beginning of the industrial era because human activity has added to the burden of CO_2e ('carbon dioxide equivalent' – mainly carbon dioxide but with other ingredients present) in the earth's atmosphere, the increase spiking upwards most sharply since the middle of the twentieth century, and even more so again since 1990. The chief culprit is the burning of fossil fuels for energy to power industry and transport, and to heat and light homes and businesses. The 'fossils' in fossil fuels are the remains of plants and marine animals fossilized over hundreds of millions of years, trees and other plants turning into coal and marine animals turning into oil and gas.[2] Plants and animals capture and store energy from the sun; burning their fossilized remains releases ancient solar energy. The remains are non-renewable and finite in quantity, so they are a diminishing resource. That is a problem in itself, but of course the immediate and far more serious problem is that burning fossils causes an excess of CO_2e in the atmosphere, creating a greenhouse – a hothouse – effect, with the result that what on the face of it look like 'modest' rises in average global temperature of 2° Celsius and above threaten highly significant adverse changes to sea levels and weather patterns – and therefore the viability of the earth's current flora and fauna, including humans.

For the first time in the planet's history the change in the global climate, and the effects this is having, are the result of the activities of a single, numerous, highly active, and highly destructive species: human beings. There have been mass extinctions before – five so far, in each of which around 75–95 per cent of species vanished. The first occurred 450 million years ago, the latest (barring the one currently in process) happened 66 million years ago – this being the Cretaceous–Paleogene extinction in which all non-avian dinosaur species were annihilated. Such wholesale extinctions meant that the planet's ecological systems had to start over, acting upon and in turn being shaped by new species arising. With the single exception of the Cretaceous–Paleogene extinction, which was caused by a major meteor impact, these extinction events were the result of climate change – specifically, climate change caused by greenhouse gases.

The worst was the Permian–Triassic or 'Great Dying' event of 250 million years ago, which annihilated more than 80 per cent of marine and 70 per cent of terrestrial life. Greenhouse gases were a major cause. Ocean warming caused a massive release of methane by destabilizing the stores of solid methane hydrates on the ocean floor; methane is a potent and fast-acting greenhouse gas, and it is found not only in oceans but in the vast regions of permafrost in earth's northern hemisphere, which, as it thaws in response to temperature rises, threatens to release its currently trapped methane. Humanity is currently releasing greenhouse gases into the atmosphere at a rate ten times faster than happened in the 'Great Dying'.

Research based on ice cores takes our knowledge of climate history back 800,000 years. There is now about 35 per cent more carbon in the atmosphere than at any point in that stretch of time, and it is hypothesized that this applies for any point in a much longer stretch – as much as the last 15 million years.

There is a chilling fact about the rate at which greenhouse gases are entering the atmosphere. The sharp rise in their presence there has, as noted, a definite and recognizable starting point: industrialization in the nineteenth century. The uptake of effective new technologies tends to be rapid; the printing press in the fifteenth century and the mobile phone at the end of the twentieth century are cases in point. Steam power, factory production, electricity generation, and automotive transport mushroomed with increasing speed in the century following the end of the Napoleonic Wars, the energy resources powering them being coal and, later, oil also – fossil fuels whose burning pumped CO_2 into the sky in huge and ever-increasing volumes, and continues to do so at ever-greater rates. In total, 85 per cent of the greenhouse gas now in the atmosphere has been emitted since the end of the Second World War. The chilling fact is that over half the volume of gases thus pumped into the sky *has been emitted since 1990*.

The greenhouse effect of CO_2e emissions has been known for a long time. The relationship between the atmosphere and global temperature was first discussed by Joseph Fourier in his *Mémoire sur les températures du globe terrestre* in 1824. At the end of the nineteenth century the Swedish physicist Svante Arrhenius (his 1903 Nobel Prize was, however, awarded for chemistry) worked out that earth's surface temperature would rise between 5° and 6° Celsius if the amount of CO_2 then present in the atmosphere were doubled. His colleague Arvid Högbom calculated that in the 1890s carbon emissions from industrial processes equalled that from all natural sources. But it was not until the 1950s that systematic monitoring of atmospheric carbon dioxide levels began, at the instigation of geologist and oceanographer Roger Revelle and his colleagues at the Scripps Institution of Oceanography in San Diego. They sited their measuring instruments at the Mauna Loa Observatory in Hawaii and in Antarctica so that greenhouse gas quantities could be determined in places least affected by local conditions of emission. Revelle reported the findings to Congress; the first use of the expression 'global warming', together with an outline of its effects on weather and the risks it posed of desertification and sea level rises, appeared in a newspaper article, published in November 1957, about the work done by Revelle and his colleagues.[3]

Revelle died in 1991. It is in the years since then that CO_2e emissions have doubled over the preceding period of increase.

At this rate average global temperature will rise by 4° Celsius by the last year of the twenty-first century. The result will be to make great tracts of North and South America, Africa, and Asia south of latitude 60° (the line of latitude that runs immediately south of the Shetland Islands, Greenland, and Siberia) uninhabitable or almost wholly so. It is already the case that the survival of existing plant and animal species requires that they move 1,000 metres a year towards the poles to keep within the habitable conditions to which they are adapted. Losses of habitats and declines in numbers of many species have already reached emergency levels. When the Paris Agreement on climate change was signed by 195 countries in April 2016, the threshold of a CO_2e atmospheric concentration of 400 ppm (parts per million) – which scientists and activists had for decades been arguing was the upper limit of tolerability – had already been passed. It is now, at time of writing, in excess of 411 ppm; in April 2021 a measurement at Mauna Loa registered a frightening 420 ppm.[4]

It is not merely possible but necessary to bring imagination to bear on the practical meaning of climate change. It has been remarked that one of the factors promoting populism in a number of Western democracies in the first and especially second decades of the twentieth century was immigration. Immigration is a phenomenon of both push and pull; migrants are pushed from their homelands by hardships, and they are pulled by the attractions of wealthy peaceful countries where opportunities for themselves and their children are greater. The hardships that push them are caused by conflicts, by repeated extreme weather events causing droughts or floods which destabilize water and food resources, and by the tension between rising populations and subsistence levels of poverty, all the factors typically operating jointly. Climate change will dramatically intensify both the push and the pull factors – and, in fact, is already doing so. Europe experienced a shock when a million refugees fled from the brutal conflict in Syria and sought asylum in European Union states. But this is small beer in comparison to what climate change will do. Consider Bangladesh, a country of 163 million people. On current warming trends, it is predicted that by 2050 up to 20 million of its people will be flooded out by rising sea levels. In 2016 more than that number were displaced by extreme weather events worldwide, most of the displacement being temporary; but in the low-lying delta regions of Bangladesh which will be lost under water, the effect will be permanent.

According to a World Bank estimate, what threatens Bangladesh will be repeated in many places on all continents, risking permanent displacement of 140 million people. That estimate is at the very low end of projections. The United Nations predicts 200 million climate refugees on optimistic assumptions, a *billion* refugees if worst fears are realized.[5] It is wise to take pessimistic projections seriously, because in working to undershoot them by as much as possible one can thereby mitigate and adapt far better to what current projections admit is already on the way: more frequent and more devastating storms, hurricanes, tornadoes, and monsoons; the drowning of some islands and coastal cities or their repeated serious flooding; heatwaves that kill people; droughts and desertification; the spread of disease-bearing insects such as mosquitoes and ticks into regions currently free of them; mushrooming populations of rats and other vermin; increasing frequency and spread of epidemic diseases, malaria, and dengue fever; interruptions in power supplies; interruptions in production and delivery of food together with outright shortages; problems with fresh water supply; damage to roads, railways, and airports; rising social and political tensions attending these stresses; and civil and international conflicts as a result.

This apocalyptic vision is not an overstatement. Disrupted weather patterns that tip the balance into drought and flood do it in easily predictable ways, because we have examples of them already. In prolonged dry spells heatwaves can be fatal for humans, water supplies are put at risk, and dust storms occur that damage topsoil and harm agriculture with resulting loss of both crops and livestock. The knock-on effect on food supplies and, in their turn, on social stability, is serious – just imagine if the supermarkets in your town had empty shelves and no prospect of restocking; how long would it be before hungry people started breaking into other people's houses in the hopes of finding hoarded tins of food? When extreme wet weather, unusually high tides, and rising sea levels cause flooding the immediate danger is that people will drown, be stranded, or be displaced as refugees; but they add further risks such as contamination of water supplies by fouling them with soil and debris and pushing sewage back out of pipes and lavatories, salinating the soil so that it becomes useless to agriculture, and leaving behind increased mould, waterborne diseases, and breeding opportunities for mosquitoes. Rising sea levels put at risk a number of highly populous cities: Dhaka, Miami, Mumbai, Sydney, Rio de Janeiro, New York, Los Angeles, Hong Kong, Shanghai, and many more. Whole regions – among them the Ganges and Nile deltas, most of Florida, the Maldives, and a number of Pacific islands – are at risk of disappearing under the sea.

While humans face the additional problems of air pollution and disease proliferation arising from these developments, other species face the results of ocean acidification, deforestation, thawing of polar ice and permafrost, and associated destruction of habitats; and most non-human species apart from the likes of rats and cockroaches are not very adaptable. Consider the polar bear, as the North Pole ice cap melts, or the gorilla, as its forest home shrinks around it before the rapid encroachment of humans seeking land to grow food as current land becomes inhospitable to agriculture. The gorilla's fate will be sealed if heat and desertification drive people further into the already-dwindled highlands that are the gorilla's home.

In the face of threats to humankind, some will regard the loss of many animal and plant species as a side show. To think so is a bad mistake. The planet is a single organism, an interconnected system forming a single ecology. Human activity distorts it, and is in the process of breaking it completely: a million animal species – 20 per cent of the total – and 40 per cent of the world's plant species are now close to extinction.[6] Biodiversity matters because it maintains the system of interdependencies that link the chain of life all the way up from bacteria to plant and animal life to the composition of the air in the earth's atmosphere. But attention is often sharpened by considering what the world stands to lose, and soon, as the mayhem continues. There are only 3,000 tigers left in the wild. Warming in the Himalayas is driving the precarious population of snow leopards higher and into more isolated pockets. Images of polar bears struggling across breaking ice floes are already familiar; less so is the fact that almost all the world's coral reefs are set to vanish when, as will soon and unstoppably happen, the global average temperature nears the 2° Celsius point. Note that these examples are of the edge places, the ones already crumbling in the rising heat: polar regions, jungle and mountain habitats, the sea. The dark mischief of warming is encroaching from these liminal zones towards us in our cities and homes.[7]

We can see satellite images of shrinking ice caps, and television footage of the increasing number and severity – and earlier onset – of wildfires ravaging Australia and California. Such examples are educative: seeing is believing, it is said. But one should pause for a moment to reflect on the serious dereliction by governments and people everywhere: these harms were predicted decades ago, science showed that carbon dioxide persists in the atmosphere for very long periods and that although warming might be slowed a little if drastic measures are taken, it will inexorably continue for a very long time yet – the rate and quantity with which humankind has burned fossil fuels has set in motion changes that will continue to unfold for thousands of years.[8] We have let this happen. We have done a very stupid thing.

The Paris Agreement specified 2° Celsius as the upper ceiling, the aim being to limit the temperature rise to 1.5° Celsius if possible, and 'as soon as possible'.[9] These figures are benchmarked against pre-industrial atmospheric concentrations of CO_2e. The plan agreed was for a series of increasingly ambitious five-year action steps to be carried out by countries. Plans for these 'nationally determined contributions' were to be submitted by 2020. The slow progress made by that date prompted US President Biden's climate envoy, John Kerry, to call on the twenty countries that between them produce over 80 per cent of global emissions to act *immediately* to cut them to zero.[10] This would help to realize the best hopes for mitigating the effects of warming. But note what, on this best hope, those effects would still nevertheless be: continuing degradation of habitats, continuing loss of species, continuing shrinking of ice sheets and vanishing of coral reefs, and continuing increases in the number and severity of extreme weather events, including lengthy heatwaves not just in already hot countries but in what have usually been temperate ones, causing thousands of extra deaths every summer.[11]

Such is the promise of the best hope of 2° Celsius or less. But the world is actually on course for 3° Celsius or more. Central

America and the Caribbean are set for long droughts; northern Africa for droughts lasting five years or more; Spain, Italy, and Greece for permanent drought. Wildfires will burn anything between twice and six times the area they destroy at present, depending on region; double around the Mediterranean, sixfold in the United States. All the worst-case outcomes described above will occur – by 2100, note; but after that the climate will still keep on warming, the consequences will keep on getting worse. The extreme example of planetary warming is Venus, a dead planet thought to be once rather similar to earth but killed by a runaway greenhouse effect a billion years ago.[12]

It should at this point be mentioned that the 'worst case' envisioned in the foregoing is a rise of 4° Celsius by the end of the century. It has now to be admitted that this is not actually *the absolute worst-case* scenario, given that if we do nothing at all to deal with carbon emissions, and simply carry on as we have been doing for the last three decades, global temperature will rise twice as much as that: by 8° Celsius![13] The effects of this are unthinkable. Most of the planet would be too hot to live in, little of it would sustain agriculture, tropical diseases would infest what are currently the polar regions, 70 per cent of today's biggest cities would be under water – and so on. Even the gloomiest of prognosticators think, fortunately, that we will not be there by 2100. But the too-likely 4° Celsius rise is not that much less bad from the point of view of the damage done and difficulties caused – the difference is like that between dying in agony and dying in extreme agony.

The question to be asked is, how has humanity allowed itself to get to this point, a quarter of the way to 2100 with the problem of CO_2e emissions not fully addressed? The answer has several parts, the most obvious being application of the negative corollary of the self-interest Law, that *what can be done will not be done if it brings costs or disadvantage to those who can stop it.* The 'those' in this case are governments and major businesses reluctant to fall behind in competition with rivals. But it is not simply a matter of foot-dragging and reluctance. There have been active and conscious efforts at denial, distortion, distraction, and delay, an unforgivable jumble of activities by both public and private agencies, leaving to future generations the task of suffering the consequences and, if they can, cleaning up the consequences of present scrambles for profit and advantage. Bluntly, this is unforgivable.

The most eloquent account of the deniers' and distracters' efforts has been given by climate scientist Michael E. Mann, himself the subject of their attacks.[14] In his book *The New Climate War* he points out that the fossil fuel industry has long been aware of the 'potentially catastrophic' effects of carbon dioxide release from burning coal and oil; an ExxonMobil scientist called James F. Black warned his company of the risks – the words 'potentially catastrophic' are his – in the 1970s, and said that unless something were done *within a decade from then* the harm would be irreversible. The response of the fossil fuel industry to the warnings of their own experts was not to act on them but to suppress them, and – even worse – to rebut them and act to forestall efforts to control CO_2e emissions.

A principal technique of those who wish to escape accountability for the effects of what they do, whether in the form of regulation, legal action, adverse publicity, loss of revenues, or anything else untoward from their point of view, is to deflect attention from those effects and themselves. Mann cites the example of the US gun lobby's 'Guns Don't Kill People, People Kill People' slogan, dating back to the period immediately after the First World War, in the Prohibition era of gang warfare in which machine guns were a weapon of choice for criminals. The infamous Second Amendment to the US Constitution, which accords a 'right to bear arms' – Supreme Court decisions as to whether this is a right of militias or individuals have oscillated back and forth – was adopted at a time, namely the year 1791, when 'arms' were muzzle-loading muskets and flintlock pistols, weapons with which it would be impossible to commit mass shootings and school massacres. The brilliant success of the gun lobby in today still being able to place hundreds of thousands of guns, among them high-powered automatic weapons, into hands many of which are unfit to be anywhere near them, is testament to the efficacy of the techniques Mann describes. More than 100 people a day die at the muzzle of a gun in the US at time of writing, four an hour. In 2017 there were 11,000 gun deaths in the US; in the UK in the same year there were 33, equivalent to 198 such deaths if scaled proportionally to account for the difference in population. The gun lobby's success in shifting all responsibility to individuals while bearing none themselves makes Mann's point with stark clarity.

The same technique undermined early efforts to deal with environmental pollution. Half a century ago, in what seemed to be a public-spirited campaign to encourage people to stop littering, a poignant advertisement in which a Native American – the 'Crying Indian' – grieves because of the despoliation of the countryside by growing tons of rubbish, was funded by the manufacturers of those very same discarded bottles, cans, and packages which constituted the growing tons of rubbish. The manufacturers' aim was to make individuals take their rubbish home or put it in litter bins – very good – but thereby they displaced responsibility from themselves wholly onto consumers. The aim was to avoid legislation that would require them to recover bottles and cans or make packaging biodegradable, the motive of course being to avoid the costs involved.

Mann's point in citing these examples is that the same strategy is being funded, to the tune of hundreds of billions of dollars, by fossil fuel interests determined to escape regulatory burdens and the loss of revenues that would follow very large-scale shifts of public funding and facilitation to renewable energy. Earlier, these interests sought to *deny* that climate change was happening, or that it was anthropogenic, or that CO_2e emissions were responsible for it, or that the effects of warming would be harmful. The science and the growing global problems have pulled the carpet from beneath that strategy. So now they seek to *deflect*, in the manner of the gun and bottle lobbies, by putting the onus on voluntary action by individuals. Become a vegan, give up flying, go to work by bike, recycle your waste, shower less often, buy local – every choice from light bulbs and soap to lifestyle in general is to be determined by its impact on the climate. All these are good things; even if there were no climate emergency they would be good things. To live mindfully, in greater harmony with what is natural and consistent with the good of others including other species and the environment itself, is obviously and unquestionably desirable. But even if every individual were to act in this way, it would not be enough, and it distracts attention – which is what the polluters want – from legislative action.[15]

The amounts of money invested by the fossil fuel industry in its endeavour to escape its responsibilities may seem very large until one reflects on the relation of those amounts to industry profits. Consider just the oil industry. The world's oil industry has made profits of over $2 trillion dollars since 1990 – that's $2,000,000,000,000 *profit*, not turnover. Money paid out for advertisements, politicians, and consultants who will gainsay expert opinion or qualify it with doubt, will be regarded as a cost of business; paying for the deflection effort does not come out of profits, it protects them.[16] Moreover consider the oil wells, refineries, tankers at sea, thousands of petrol (gas) stations, and numbers of employees involved. Consider that in the US alone nearly 10 million people are directly or indirectly dependent on the oil industry for their livelihoods, and the reluctance of government to impose stringent obligations on the oil industry to address their climate responsibilities scarcely needs the lobbyists' fees, the donations to political election coffers, the pork-barrel promises to invest or spend in a given lawmaker's congressional district or state, to persuade politicians not to hold the oil industry to account.

'Qualify with doubt'; Mann quotes a tobacco industry internal memo about how to handle the threat to its profits from the cigarette link to lung cancer: 'doubt is our product'. Sow a doubt, and it will be an excuse to those addicted to nicotine to ignore science's warnings; sow a doubt, and regulators will be hesitant to intervene in case the warnings are wrong or exaggerated.[17]

Another aim of the fossil fuel industry is to divide those against them. The chief achievable split is between those who urge individual action and those who insist that only major policy changes, requiring collective action, will be sufficient. Social media platforms have been a godsend to them in this regard. To get bitter and highly divisive arguments going, a few trolls and bots artfully insinuating hostile remarks and charges of dishonesty, stupidity, and bigotry quickly set snowballs rolling, and people concerned about the plight of the planet are soon fighting each other instead of the enemy.

Recognizing that there are many people not party to this furore and still undecided or only mildly engaged, the industry uses other 'psy-ops' techniques, variously pitched. One tactic is to argue that climate change effects will be minor. Another is to say that they can only be tackled by extreme measures such as overthrowing capitalism. A third is to say it is too late and nothing can be done. In these ways action can be paralysed or misdirected, confused, and undermined – in sum: hampered.

At the same time as all this, the pro-fossil lobbies work hard to stop regulation, to discredit renewable energy options, to promote fixes such as 'clean coal', and to float schemes whose cost and technological challenges put them into the zone of unfeasibility in the short and medium term, such as geo-engineering. The last resort is to say that things are already so bad we must just hope and pray that a brilliant technological solution will emerge from the pressure to find one, and that meanwhile we must keep industry going, keep jobs, keep generating the wealth which the new technological fix, when discovered, will need by way of investment.

Just how quickly and easily climate defence efforts can be rolled back is illustrated by the four dire years of the Trump presidency. Right from his election campaign in 2016 Trump declared himself a climate change sceptic, and the consequences were predictable once he was in office. The US's Environmental Protection Agency's Clean Power Plan was unpicked and replaced with the Affordable Clean Energy rule which set no emission reduction goals and left it to individual states to decide how to regulate power plant emissions. The Agency issued permissions for laying pipelines – most notably the Keystone XL pipeline – and for oil prospecting on public lands, facilitating the endeavour with cheap leases.[18] It simultaneously handed subsidies to the declining coal industry, many of whose employees were Trump voters. Fuel efficiency standards were weakened, reducing the pressure on vehicle manufacturers to develop clean technology, and the waiver allowing California to set stricter vehicle emission standards than those nationally mandated was withdrawn. Changes were made to rules governing how much methane – that highly dangerous and rapid-acting greenhouse gas – could be emitted from landfills and from oil and gas extraction processes. This list is incomplete. Between them Trump's measures threatened an additional 400 million tons of emissions by 2030 than Obama's plans had allowed for, together with an extra 850,000 tons of methane.[19]

It is a speculation, but a plausible one, that interests that were well aware of Trump's deficiencies nevertheless saw in them opportunities to hinder what they regarded, from their own viewpoint, as negative developments. Having a bull in the china shop distracting everyone is handy if you want to pick the lock on the shop's safe. Many more than just the fossil fuel interests might have been happy to see Trump in the White House, but his presence there was certainly a gain to the fossil fuel industry and a setback for the world's climate.

Within the framework of Trump's climate policies both the gain and the setback were temporary. But the slow and faltering progress towards implementing the Paris Agreement of 2016 is more serious. Even so, hope remains that something can be done. Michael Mann and Bill Gates are among those who have offered ways forward.

Mann offers a 'four-point battle plan'. The first point is that the doomsayers must be ignored; it is not too late to act. To leave unchallenged what doomsayers say simply allows the fossil fuel industry to continue with business as usual, because the effort to constrain them and to find clean energy alternatives will be abandoned if their pessimistic message is believed. The second point is that great hope lies with today's young people, 'fighting tooth and nail to save their planet . . . there is a moral authority and clarity in their message that none but the most jaded ears can fail to hear.'[20] This is emphatically true. Greta Thunberg, the Extinction Rebellion activists, and all those whom they inspire, rightly refuse to accept that nothing can be done.

The third point is to 'educate, educate, educate'.[21] Whereas there is no point in engaging with hard-core deniers whose minds will not be changed, there is everything to be gained by informing people, correcting misinformation, challenging the messages that deniers and distracters purvey, and encouraging people to join the effort.

The final point is that 'changing the system requires systemic change'.[22] The greatest part of the solution lies with policy, with government and international action. This in turn requires mobilization of collective efforts to elect governments that will act, and remove governments that will not act.

Bill Gates's view is likewise that solutions have to lie at the level of policy: we have to 'revolutionize the world's physical economy – and that will take, among other things, a dramatic infusion of ingenuity, funding, and focus from . . . government. No one else has the resources to drive the research we need.'[23] His plan is to 'expand the supply of innovations' and 'accelerate the demand for innovations' directed at eliminating carbon emissions to achieve a zero-carbon goal by 2050. The first is a research and development drive, bringing science and engineering together to create zero-emission technologies. The list of these is long. One is producing hydrogen without emitting carbon – hydrogen is a clean fuel whose waste-product is water; at present getting it into usable form generates too much CO_2. Others are long-term grid-scale electricity storage; biofuels and electrofuels; production of steel, concrete, plastics, and fertilizers without carbon emissions; next-generation nuclear fission, nuclear fusion, hydro power, geothermal energy, and thermal storage; food crops resistant to drought and flood; meat alternatives; and carbon capture.

To get these technologies, the necessity is appropriate levels of direct public investment. At present R&D spending is nugatory, only 0.02 per cent of the global economy. The US government spends $7 billion on clean energy development, whereas a more realistic target would involve matching the $37 billion budget of the National Institutes of Health.[24] And bold ideas need to be backed, with the level and security of funding that will allow researchers to achieve breakthroughs, especially where these are matched to identified practical needs. Bringing the public and private sectors together, universities and industry, right from the beginning of the process through to completion, will overcome a problem Gates identifies, namely, the idea that governments fund early-stage innovation and industry carries the baton forward thereafter.[25] This slows the innovation cycle and introduces the risk-aversion that attends caution about effects on the bottom line.

Gates acknowledges that the second part of his recipe, namely, acceleration of demand for innovations – which means achieving the requisite levels of take-up and application of new technologies – is more challenging. The new technologies have to prove their efficacy and cost-effectiveness in the real world. That means keeping costs and risks as low as possible, and making consumers comfortable with what is on offer. Take 'meat alternatives' as an example of what is involved in the latter; it is one thing to persuade people to switch to biofuel use, another to persuade them to eat laboratory-produced meat or plant-based meat lookalikes. Investors are deterred by the uncertainties attached to bringing novelties like this to market. The cost of switching to low-carbon technologies has the same effect; in both cases major changes in consumers' behaviour are required, and their resistance or rejection would be expensive, even bankrupting.

A solution to this is 'procurement power', the power of governments to buy very large quantities of energy and construction materials. Gates cites the example of militaries buying low-carbon fuels for ships and planes, local and national government using low-carbon cement and steel in construction, and utilities investing in low-carbon power and storage. Governments can also invest in the infrastructure needed: 'transmission lines for wind and solar, charging stations for electric vehicles, pipelines for captured carbon'.[26] And they can provide enablement through regulatory frameworks too. The scale of the purchases drives down costs, and at the same time effects savings elsewhere in national budgets from the health and social benefits accrued. This, Gates points out, is how the internet got going; it had a major buyer – the US government.[27]

In addition to governments 'shaping the market' by these means there is the major benefit of the message thus sent and the example thus set. But there have to be other forms of direct intervention that specifically target the problem: carbon pricing, either through a carbon tax or a cap-and-trade system, and imposing clean energy and product standards, a familiar example of which in the domestic sphere is energy-saving light bulbs. Legislation requiring all surface vehicles to be electrically powered by a given year would be a significant move in the same vein.[28]

Although international cooperation on these measures is essential, the public sector has many levels at which action can be taken, from local, state, and provincial governments to the national government. These latter are in a position to engage with other governments in agreeing to act cooperatively, which includes ensuring that poorer countries can have access to green technologies too, bearing in mind that their efforts to raise populations out of poverty and to provide health, education, and employment put them at a disadvantage which would be unjust if not addressed. This is 'not charity'; it is of ultimate benefit to all.[29] The example of sharing medical knowledge and vaccine technology for dealing with the Covid-19 pandemic is a direct parallel.

The call to governments to step up investment with the aim of achieving zero carbon emissions by 2050 looked as if it had found a response in the Biden administration when it came into office at the beginning of 2021. President Biden immediately signed executive orders saying that he would 'listen to the science' and hear the 'cry for survival' from the planet. Actions matched words; the US rejoined the Paris accord, revoked a raft of Trump's environmentally damaging executive orders including cancelling the XL pipeline, reimposing the moratorium on drilling in the Arctic, and pausing all new permits and leases for drilling both offshore and on federal lands. He instructed all federal agencies to aim for a carbon-free electricity sector by 2035, and set up an Office of Domestic Climate Policy, a national climate advisor, a special presidential envoy for the climate (John Kerry), and a Civilian Climate Corps. And in addition to ordering that all federal agencies must work to reduce climate pollution 'in every sector of the environment', he declared an aim of ending international financing of fossil fuels. One of the most striking initiatives was a commitment to climate justice and protection of communities of colour which had been disproportionately harmed by polluters.

Although there were immediate criticisms saying that some of these steps were in reality only half-steps – why 'pause' permits and leases and not simply ban them? – there was also widespread welcome for the signal of intent thus sent. But the real cause for concern, as Ben Ehrenreich argued in the *New*

Republic in March 2021 – less than three months after these sweeping measures were announced – is that they are not enough to prevent catastrophe. Large and vocal choruses of scientists have repeatedly argued that radical measures are needed, in comparison to which these are sticking plasters. Ehrenreich reminded readers that in 2019 eleven thousand scientists from 150 countries had signed a 'Warning of a Climate Emergency', repeating the call to arms of the 'Warning to Humanity' signed by fifteen thousand scientists in 2017. By 'radical' the call means *radical*: 'fundamental changes to global capitalism, education, and equality, which include *inter alia* the abolition of perpetual economic growth'.[30] In effect the criticism of the Biden initiatives is that they try to have a cake and eat it: growth, jobs, business as usual, on the one hand, and saving the planet on the other. But scientists' warning is that the two are inconsistent. The hope, or perhaps better the wish, that a 'green transition' is possible to make the two consistent is known as 'decoupling' – preserving the current growth-oriented model of economic activity from having to change by breaking the link between it and environmental considerations. The basic concept is in effect Bill Gates's idea: clean up the energy and technology that drives the model. The same assumption underlies the 2018 report by the IPCC which, though unequivocally stating that if 'net zero' is not reached by 2050 there will be a cataclysm, nevertheless did not envisage a change in the rate of economic growth over the same period. Ehrenreich quoted Fredric Jameson: 'it is easier to imagine the end of the world than the end of capitalism'.

One reason for Ehrenreich's pessimism about Gates-style solutions is that nothing like them has succeeded before. Another is that changes in the climate and their cumulative effects are not linear, but mutually potentiating and saltatory

– happening in sudden jumps upon reaching tipping points, with cascading consequences: for example, instantaneous mass release of methane from thawing permafrost, huge glaciers and ice sheets collapsing, sudden disruption of an ecological system by the swift demise of a species – think what would happen if bee and butterfly populations vanished in just a few years; at time of writing, anxiety over bee numbers in Europe and the plummeting numbers of migrating monarch butterflies in North America are cases in point.

Reducing emissions by itself is not enough, and current plans, like those advanced by President Biden, envision reduction not cessation; so removal of CO_2 from the atmosphere has to be part of the story. As noted, carbon capture and storage offer technological challenges, and proposals to offset emissions by forest planting are over-optimistic: ActionAid calculated that there is simply not enough land available to accommodate all of the tree planting proposed by corporations and governments as offsets and carbon sinks. 'To save this planet,' Ehrenreich remarks, 'it appears we'll need another one. This is what currently counts as pragmatism.'[31]

Perhaps the most significant claim in criticisms of the attempt to maintain today's economic status quo while saving the planet nonetheless – that is, to achieve the 'decoupling' effort – is that the concept of *growth* has to be challenged. 'As innocuous as it may sound, "growth" should be understood to describe the frenzied ruination of nearly every ecosystem on the planet so that its richest human inhabitants can hold on to their privileges for another generation or two.'[32] There are dreadful ironies in this situation. The production, processing, and transport of food accounts for almost half of all greenhouse gas emissions, yet a quarter of US children, and even more in the world at large, do not have food security, and epidemics of malnourishment and obesity coexist as the environment suffers and thousands of species plummet to extinction.

The note of sometimes angry pessimism in Ehrenreich's account suggests an assumption of his own; that attitudes are unlikely to change fast enough for action of the required kind and scale to be taken. With this Gates and others disagree. Gates sees a shift in the weight of sentiment, bringing a tipping point closer. This is true of public opinion: he cites the positive movement in polling data between 2015 and 2020, and points out that both coal and gas use are in a downward spiral.[33] Equally significant is the sign that banks and finance houses are increasingly switching from fossil fuel to green energy investments. They are not doing it wholly out of charitable feeling; fossil fuel investments progressively lose their value as the switch to green continues. But many younger investors have livelier consciences, and the prospect of shareholders insisting on the fiduciary responsibility of corporations to act in their shareholder interests – which include protection of the planet – could see legal pressures, or the prospect of them, changing minds and therefore practice. As with the climate and its effects themselves, there are tipping points in human affairs.

Nevertheless, as the Covid-19 pandemic so tragically demonstrated, delay is dangerous. Talk of target dates of 2030 and 2050 are temptations to procrastinators; 'next year' is the corporate or governmental *mañana*. Carbon pricing, abolishing fossil fuel subsidies and incentives, and investing vigorously and copiously in renewable energy and other technological desiderata as identified by Gates, are necessary right away.

On the equally important point of climate justice in a world so sharply divided between rich and poor nations, Ehrenreich cited the 'Emissions Gap Report' from the UN Environment Programme which contains a calculation that warming could be held to 1.5° Celsius if the richest 1 per cent reduced their emissions by a factor of 30, which would allow the world's poorest half to *treble* its per capita emissions, taking its populations above want and struggle to acceptable standards of living. Ehrenreich adds, 'Billionaires who drop to one-thirtieth of their fortunes are still multimillionaires.'[34]

Broadly speaking, the options available to humanity are: either break the negative version of the self-interest Law (*what can be done will not be done*) by radically switching direction from a growth model to a sustainability model of economic activity, or make the decoupling agenda work – that is, find the fixes that would make renewable energy cheap and plentiful, would remove and safely store the excess CO_2e in the atmosphere, and would positively incentivize doing both. At time of writing the first option is not in play and the second is a mixture of insufficiencies and wishful thinking.

Most of the insufficiencies are on the right track: renewable green energy generation using wind, solar, and hydro has become not merely feasible but progressively cheaper, to the extent that the International Energy Agency World Energy Outlook for 2020 declared that solar-generated electricity is 'the cheapest source of electricity in history'.[35] But although in some places there is progress, overall it is mostly slow. In 2019 renewables accounted for 11 per cent of all primary energy sources, in the US between 5 and 10 per cent, and between 10 and 20 per cent in Europe and China. The stand-out region is Scandinavia, with between 50 per cent and 85 per cent of its primary energy recruited from renewables.[36] Obviously, the overall 11 per cent is nowhere near enough. Equally obviously, these technologies, plus those harvesting energy from geothermal and tidal activity, have proven themselves and are a major way to go; investment is set to increase in all of them, but the quantum is the key issue – which is why substantial direct public investment and strong incentives for private investment are essential.

Correlatively, more efficient energy *use* is needed. There are large savings to be made from the design of buildings to the devices used to heat, light, and transport people. Although the introduction of energy-saving devices has resulted in a drop in domestic consumption in some places (for example, the UK) of as much as 50 per cent since the beginning of the twenty-first century, in Europe buildings take 40 per cent of overall energy and are responsible for 35 per cent of emissions. There is a large distance still to travel towards sustainability.

A weight of expert opinion says that given the urgent need to limit warming to less than 2° Celsius by 2050, measures additional to these are needed. Carbon capture and sequestration is one such. The technology for it exists, and at time of writing it is being implemented, albeit in small and patchy ways.

Limiting methane emissions from cattle farming is another; either red seaweed fodder, or isolation of the ingredient in it which reduces methane in bovine eructation (which red seaweed does by 80 per cent), would help.

An alternative to the seaweed fix is to replace beef altogether with other sources of protein. Textured soy and other vegetable proteins are already used to mimic meat, and it is argued that insects such as mealworms are a good if initially rebarbative possibility – they are already acceptable in some cultures, and require much less land and water than cattle farming. Given the destructive deforestation that accompanies cattle farming, the insect option is less unrealistic than it seems: one either chooses it in manageable ways, or has it thrust upon one in less palatable ways by the necessity to survive in the aftermath of systemic ecological and economic collapse.

Various forms of geo-engineering and 'climate repair' suggestions – refreezing the polar regions by brightening the cloud layer over them, encouraging submarine plant growth to absorb more CO_2, afforestation schemes on an extensive scale to serve as carbon sinks (but recall ActionAid's scepticism about land availability) – are among other suggestions. Various climate-cooling and weather-influencing ideas are mooted, ranging from the perhaps-feasible-with-difficulty to the pure-science-fiction; at present they generate more controversy than either clean energy or progress.

These ideas figure among the sought-for 'technical fixes' that some are keen to warn us against relying on, and which Gates says must be backed and promoted in the hope that at least some of them may prove not just feasible but effective. The rapid development and deployment of vaccines in the Covid-19 pandemic are a hopeful augury that this is not an empty approach. Provided that one does not *merely* bank on them by continuing with business as usual in the hopes that one of the fixes will pop out of the blue sky and save us, there is every reason to encourage the Gates approach – alongside challenging the destructive growth model that has brought the problem upon us; for business as usual is indeed not an option, and working to mitigate and prepare for the effects of the warming already unavoidable, together with increasing efforts to cut both energy consumption and CO_2e emissions, remains mandatory.

What can individuals do? Individual involvement is vital, because although it cannot be enough by itself it is an important adjunct to the overall endeavour. The main and most obvious respect is the pressure that individuals acting collectively (no paradox here) exert on governments. In the ideal, the voting public could elect a government committed to all-out climate policies, taxing emissions, incentivizing green energy, investing in the technologies and infrastructure for the latter and for carbon capture and sequestration, using its procurement strength, its legislative competence, and its direct interventions to redefine the landscape. Above all, the needed shift from a single and relentless focus on growth to sustainability and social justice – the two have to be linked to ensure that the costs of redistribution in economic effort do not fall disproportionately on those less advantageously placed at the starting point – has to be a plank of such policies. Above all, the need for concerted global action requires that governments work together, not dragging their feet to preserve as much competitive advantage as they can; voters can force governments to break the self-interest Law.

This ideal is not impossible to achieve, but it is difficult as an immediate prospect, and alas unlikely until the emergency has become so great that ignorers and nay-sayers are frightened into action at last. By then it might be too late, which is why, despite the difficulty, one has to keep trying. But efforts which succeed short of the ideal are still worthwhile, at very least because they buy time, and one can always both hope and aim to reach a tipping point in attitudes and practices, which would bring the ideal situation yet closer or even realize it.

Letters to government ministers and parliamentary or congressional representatives, attendance at local meetings, joining citizen groups and activist organizations, and participation in public demonstrations, are all ways to use the voice that each member of society has a right to use. Helping to raise both funds and awareness for climate campaigns is a concrete way of advancing the cause. Persuading local authorities to go green does good in itself and sends valuable signals nationally. Persuading one's

own workplace and family to do likewise demonstrates commitment. And one can stand for election on a green ticket locally or
nationally oneself; even if one is not elected, the message will
have received another public airing – and the message needs
endless restatement.

The political process is not the only target. Individuals can
bring pressure to bear on corporations. As happened in legal
actions against the tobacco industry, suing industries for damage
caused by their production of greenhouse gases can have an
influence not only in itself but in the reputational risk it causes
companies blamed for environmental and health harms, with
consequent impact on the companies' bottom-lines and share
value. Shareholders can demand that the companies in which
they invest act in environmentally responsible ways; enough of
them voting at an annual general meeting can redirect company
policy in relevant respects.

Individuals are also consumers, and how one chooses in the
supermarket makes a difference. I recall being horrified by the
extent of oil palm plantations one sees flying over Malaysia, the
world's second-largest producer of palm oil used in a wide variety of products, from soaps and shampoos to cooking ingredients to cleaning and fuel products. The reduction in biodiversity
caused by vast plantations of a single species of tree speaks for
itself; when oil palms replace rainforest and threaten orang-utan
habitats, destructiveness has gone beyond bounds. It does not
take long to read the list of ingredients on product packaging,
and to decide whether to use the power of your personal income
to make a difference.

Imagine: if everyone stopped buying products with palm oil
in them, the immense landscapes of oil palms could be returned
to native rainforest. If everyone gave up beef, the despoliation
of Amazon rainforest for ranching would stop. Of course, the

utopian possibility of wholesale changes in consumption behaviour like these is unlikely, and it is fortunate that a significant effect can still be achieved if enough people do it. This generates the free-rider problem – those who continue using palm oil products and eating beef, leaving it to others to make the difference. Now imagine what happens when everyone chooses to ride free. And consider – someone might sarcastically add – how moral, how noble, how admirable is the free-rider choice itself.

The supermarket is not the only arena for consumer choices to make a difference; one's domestic energy supplier for lighting, air conditioning, and cooking, the car one drives, and one's endeavour to offset the carbon emissions from one's business and leisure travel, by funding tree-planting activities for example, all count. And finally, one's preparedness to talk to others, to persuade and to set an example, make a difference too; altering some of someone else's behaviour by these means is a pixel in the overall picture of the battle to save the world.[37] Individual action will not solve the problem – for that, international cooperation is essential. But it can help, not least as a demonstration of opinion.

Climate change will have different physical impacts in different regions of the world, but some regions – the poorer south of the planet especially – will be especially hard hit. That means that the people least well equipped to deal with the effects will be most challenged by them. If climate change affected everyone everywhere equally, it would not be necessary to point out that if the burden of dealing with climate change is not fairly shared, citizens of richer economies will in effect be free-riding on the suffering of the poor. It might with truth be pointed out that this is already the case, given the inequities baked into the global economic system. But in the face of evermore severe droughts, floods, extreme weather events, disease, and starvation threatened by climate change, this inequity deepens.

In ethical theory one meets with the concept of 'enlightened self-interest', predicated on scepticism about the existence of genuine altruism in human motivation.[38] Let us accept this disagreeable view for a moment, and consider what 'enlightened self-interest' would mandate in the case of climate change. A collapse in world trade would seriously hit pockets in the richer, safer North. Not being able to outsource production and services to lower-cost labour markets in the poorer South would likewise impact pockets in the richer, safer North. Floods of refugees would impose social and economic burdens on the richer, safer North, amounting perhaps to civil strife, and the necessity of harsh action to prevent refugees crossing borders – refugee camps are already an ugly testimony to conflicts and genocides as well as natural disasters, and many more, some the size of huge cities, can confidently be expected if the world's temperature rises beyond 2° Celsius. The spread of diseases and vermin into the richer, safer North unused to both would impose additional burdens on health and welfare systems. Since winds, rivers, and ocean currents have no interest in national borders, and nor do air and water pollution and ocean acidification and warming, both North and South can harm each other if neither does enough, and the poorer, more vulnerable South can only do enough if the richer, more resilient North helps.

These are only a few examples, but they are enough to suggest to anyone self-interested in the richer, safer North that they are not safer and will be considerably less rich if they attempt to free-ride on the poorer South in confronting the climate challenge. The short message is that climate change will have different *physical* impacts on different regions, but a deleterious overall impact on the *whole* world nonetheless. No one and nothing will escape the consequences. So even self-interest requires addressing the climate problem for the whole world – and without delay.

There is another aspect to the question of the unfair distribution of burdens imposed by climate change. This is that its ill effects weigh most heavily on women, particularly in regions where sexual discrimination is greatest – once again, in the poorer, less resilient South. The reasons are many, and some may seem trivial but in practice are not. For example, in these regions women are more likely to be at home than out in the public domain, so when earthquakes, floods, or hurricanes occur, they are more at risk from collapsing buildings and mudslides. In many traditional societies women do not learn to swim and they wear hampering clothing, putting them at risk of drowning in floods. Because they collect water and tend crops, they are exposed to disease sources associated with water, especially standing water – malaria, dengue fever, giardiasis, schistosomiasis, typhoid, hepatitis, cryptosporidiosis, cyclosporiasis, Escherichia coli, leptospirosis – diseases caused by mosquitoes, water-borne parasites, and rat and cattle urine. Women and girls are always at risk of assault, and walking longer distances to find usable water increases the risk, as does their vulnerability in emergency situations when social order is fragile or has broken down. Managing personal hygiene is an issue for women; for example, it poses difficulties for adolescent girls if the schools they wish to attend are without toilets; such problems are exacerbated if home or village toilet facilities are destroyed.[39] The responsibility to protect and feed children and elderly dependents falls heavily on women, and in times of failed food supply women often go without to ensure that their children and elders are fed. The burden of health care is theirs too, and in difficult circumstances they will face multiple vectors of stress – food supply, sick family members, themselves at risk, the climatic conditions militating against their efforts to cope. The UN climate chief at the Paris talks in 2015, Christiana Figueres, in pointing out that women are impacted disproportionately by climate warming, reminded delegates that it is essential to involve women in discussions about how the warming challenge is to be met; elaborate efforts can come to nothing if a lynch-pin consideration is overlooked.[40]

A final point concerns the moral responsibility that presently living generations of people have to future generations. It is taken for granted that acting in such a way as to bequeath a poisoned and depleted planet to future generations – a planet more difficult to live in, with fewer resources available to manage doing so – is wrong. A counterargument to this is to say that future generations will know no different, they will not be in a position to compare the planet they find themselves in with something different and putatively better; and they might still have as many opportunities, in their own way, to have lives worth living as we or any previous generations of people have had. Indeed, the fact that they – they in particular, and not some other set of people – are alive at all will be the consequence of the choices we make today; one set of descendants will exist if we battle hard to limit global warming, another set will exist if we do nothing to battle global warming; either set will take the world as it finds it and seek the best for themselves in it. On this view, we cannot now decide on their behalf whether what we do helps or harms them in respects that matter to them.[41] It would seem to follow, unintuitively but logically, that it does not matter – at least to future generations of human beings – whether we act on global warming or not.

This counterargument leaves aside questions of our current responsibility for other species which are going extinct right now because of our activities. That is a separate point, as shown by a consideration the counterargument's upholders might advance to the effect that the extinction of non-avian dinosaurs 65 million years ago is not a deprivation for us today. Rather, the point for the upholders of the counterargument is that we are judging what constitutes benefit or harm for *future* people by *our* own lights; 'what matters to us' is what we take to license our assuming that we know what will be best for them.

There is a further consideration; if we knew that a person living in the future would be deprived of something that we possess and value now, would it therefore be better not to bring that person into existence at all, or is existence such a good in itself that it would be better for her to exist even though thus deprived?

One way to cut through the entanglements of theory that can be woven in the philosopher's study is to focus on the question of what reasons we find persuasive for acting one way rather than another now, in the present and its circumstances. With no crystal ball available in which to see what future people – whether in a blasted planet or a (relatively) saved planet – might value, given that either kind of people will have things to value, we can appeal to two kinds of considerations to guide us.

One is that *our* actions have to stand the scrutiny of *our* best lights. What we currently think is a life worth living and a planet worth having has to be the criterion for what we do about the adverse pressures we identify. What other standards can we appeal to? By hypothesis, we do not know how future people might distribute the weight of their valuations, so we cannot appeal to them; the circumstances we find ourselves in now introduce novelties that the value-system we share with predecessors (those commonalities that allow us to understand what and why they did what they did) were not *specifically* designed for, so we have to apply them adaptively. Either way we have to stand on our own resources; and by the best that we can do with them, since none other are available, our choices must be judged.

The other considerations are those revealed by experimenting with counterfactuals: if we, valuing what we value, were to be transported a hundred years into a future which has unfolded with no effort made to restrain global warming, what would we find to regret and mourn, and why? The list we make tells us what we should now address. Alternatively, we can surmise what a person living a hundred years from now in that same globally warmed future would think if transported back to the present, or – better still – to the pre-industrial environment; and the list she draws up of what she regrets has been lost (as we today might list the loss of clean air and water, quiet, greater biodiversity, more extensive wildernesses) would tell us what we need to work to save.

The weakness of the counterfactual strategy is that it ignores what might compensate for the harms caused by failing to restrain global warming. For example, in the retrospective case, the advent of modern dentistry might be regarded as a fine compensation for the increase in volume of traffic noise in our streets. If one were to fly forward to the future into a hot, depleted planet whose tropics are uninhabitable and whose polar bears and gorillas are no more, and discover that cancer, cardiovascular disease, war, and racism have been eradicated because the set of people who came into existence as a result of our not restraining the rise in global temperature proved capable of eradicating them, might we not think that the apparently Faustian bargain on climate had its compensations after all?

Implausible as this is, it illustrates the problem with the counterfactual strategy, and concentrates reliance on the first 'best
lights' strategy. But this latter, in my view, is more than adequate.
To oppose it with the *possibility* that future people might not
agree that limiting a global temperature rise was the right priority for us cannot undermine the claim that our best lights tell us
that it *is* the right priority for us. The case we have is overwhelming to us; should it transpire that we completely failed to see
something which, had we known it, would have made us act
differently, it would remain that we were acting by our best
lights, and that is the most and best we can do.[42]

One principal reason why governments are slow to act to reduce
greenhouse emissions and to convert their economies to renewable energy sources – these jointly being by far the major way to
minimize the damage – is the short-termism of the political and
economic cycle. States fear losing competitive advantage to rival
economies that do less, or act more slowly, than themselves. So
they hesitate and delay, they make promises but do not fulfil
their promises, and the global situation worsens.

In the world's general public, some people – alas, only a small
percentage – are frantic about the dangers of global warming,
and they and some others personally adopt behaviours intended
to contribute to slowing the rise in global temperature. But the
great majority of people are indifferent to the problem, or ignore
it. It is likely that almost all these latter ignore it for the reason
that they have become deadened to talk of it because the warnings have been sounded for so long; or they have become deaf-
ened and numbed by the technicalities involved; or have grate-
fully accepted the climate sceptics' views so that they can feel
relieved of any responsibility for thinking – let alone doing
anything – about it.

To say – as I argued earlier – that discussion 'should' focus on mitigation and adaptation relative to the worst-case scenario rather than more optimistic scenarios is an acknowledgement that too much energy is diverted from the efforts of climate scientists and advocates into combating the deniers, distractors, and delayers – those who deny that global warming is happening, or who deny that it is caused by human activity, or who deny that anything can be done about it, or who seek to shift responsibility for dealing with it from corporations and governments to private individuals by concentrating attention on veganism, avoiding air travel, recycling kitchen waste, and the like – all good in themselves and profoundly well-intentioned, but far from sufficient even if all individuals everywhere did it. These variously motivated attempts by deniers and distracters are deliberate. They perfectly illustrate the negative form of the self-interest Law, *what can be done will not be done if it brings costs or disadvantage to those who can stop it.* The United States under President Trump was a stand-out illustration of this law in operation; Trump withdrew the United States from the Paris climate agreement of 2016, and proudly displayed a sign saying, 'Trump digs coal'. Fortunately, he was a one-term president, and was followed by a more enlightened one.

The evidence that global warming is the result of human activity over the last couple of centuries is clear and overwhelming. Therefore the harm threatened to other species and the global environment, and to future generations of humanity, is the responsibility of previous and present generations, and imposes an additional moral obligation to act.

One has to repeat: matters have already gone so far that the world is now, at this present time, in an emergency situation. Almost all responsible contributors to the climate debate say that what we can now hope for is *at best* mitigation. This is because it is already too late to stop global warming, and efforts either to reduce the degree to which it occurs, or to find scientific solutions to halt or even reverse its effects in the hope of maintaining climate variability between predictable and manageable extremes, are at time of writing yet unsuccessful.

If better than mitigation is aimed for – as it should be – really robust action is required. A clear summary is provided by the Climate Crisis Advisory Group's June 2021 report.[43] It specifies three essentials: *reduce, remove, repair*. Reduce: to keep global warming below 2° Celsius, states have to triple their current reduction targets for greenhouse gas emissions. Remove: removing greenhouse gases from the atmosphere to bring concentrations below 350 ppm requires a range of nature-based and biomimicry carbon capture initiatives. Repair: repair already-damaged regions by strong interventions such as rewilding entire areas on land and at sea, and refreezing the polar regions by solar-radiation occlusion methods. Both the latter two desiderata involve much that is speculative. Yet if all three were done, then even though several tipping points have already been passed, climatic conditions could be stabilised and vital biodiversity and ecosystems protected for future generations.

As implied by the 'distracter' point mentioned above – relating to how the burden of effort to address climate change is shifted, by those who wish to evade responsibility for it, onto private individuals – a key consideration is this: the required action has to be international in scale, needing cooperation and agreement among the governments of the world's major economies both about what is to be done and how the cost of doing it can be fairly distributed across the all world's economies and peoples. The climate crisis is thus entangled with questions of social and international justice also; blindness to this is an obstacle to effective action.

2

TECHNOLOGY AND
THE FUTURE

Two of the most striking facts about technological developments are these: the rapidity of their take-up and spread, and the
way they potentiate further technological development, somewhat on the model of 'halving the time and doubling the power'
– halving the time to the next stage, doubling the efficacy of
what the next stage can do.[1] One could cite many examples, but
the following two will suffice.

Between the years 1436 and 1453 Johannes Gutenberg developed the technology of movable type, an innovation perfectly
suited to languages written in a limited number of alphabetic
symbols that could be arranged and rearranged to form any
word. Printing had been invented in China centuries before, but
Chinese printers had to carve thousands of individual characters, each on their own separate wood blocks, whereas movable
type meant that the same relatively few letters could be reused
repeatedly in different combinations.

Gutenberg's innovations revolutionized every part of the
process. He made the type from an alloy of lead with tin and
antimony, so durable that even after repeated use it left clear
print. He cast the type in a template matrix, making for ease of

operation and uniformity of output. And he invented an oil-based ink which was an improvement on the water-based inks used in hand-copying of texts.

Gutenberg set up his press in the city of Mainz; before the end of the fifteenth century, in less than fifty years, nearly 300 European cities had printing presses, and twenty million copies of books had poured from them. By the end of the following century that number had increased to 200 million copies.

A contemporary example is provided by mobile phones (cell phones). The very first demonstration model of a mobile phone was made in 1973 by Motorola engineers. It weighed two kilos. The first commercial mobile phone, the Motorola DynaTAC 8000X, entered the market in 1984. It took ten hours to charge and gave thirty minutes of use time. These developments were made possible by advances in semiconductor technology. The next steps involved batteries, further miniaturization of circuitry, and bandwidth availability. Japanese companies brought lithium-ion batteries to market in 1991, then in the first decade of the twenty-first century solutions to bandwidth limitations were addressed, necessitated by the increasing functionality of the devices, by development of the 4G network and beyond – roll-out of 5G began in 2019.

At time of writing, 'smartphones' have made it commonplace to access email and the internet; send texts, images, and audio files; take high-quality digital photographs and videos; play sophisticated games; and connect wirelessly through Bluetooth and infrared; all in a slim, light object that fits in a handbag or jacket pocket, and – a familiar but still astonishing fact – packing greatly more computing power than was involved in the moon landing of 1969.

'Moore's Law' is commonly cited in connection with the rapidly ballooning growth in the power of these technologies. In

1965 Gordon Moore, one of the founders of Intel and its CEO, predicted that the number of components in an integrated circuit would double every year until 1975. He underestimated the runaway success to come; at the beginning of the third decade of the twenty-first century his Law still applied. Smartphone processor chips are down to a seven nanometer scale and are set to reach five nanometers, though there is scepticism about whether transistor density can increase much beyond that – which would mean that Moore's Law would, at last, fail. The Law is not a law of science but an empirical observation, and indeed a self-fulfilling one because the industries based on the microprocessor have used it to set targets for themselves. But whether or not the inverse relationship between size and power in these technologies continues in this way, the more general point is established: that each developmental step tends to make possible yet further, and often multiple, developmental steps in a pattern more geometrical than arithmetical in sequence. 'Ballooning' is the right word.

These examples illustrate both features of the rapidity with which technologies can *spread* in take-up and *develop* in sophistication. Nor are the spread and development linear in a sense that might seem to be implied by these examples – just more printing, just more connectivity and functionality – but ideas in one field can spark ideas in other fields, by adaptation, suggestion, and analogy. A particular example is how miniaturization in mobile phone components suggested miniature medical cameras which, swallowed by patients, transmit diagnostic images from inside the body. This in turn suggests miniature and nano-scale devices capable of performing internal medical procedures, controlled remotely – perhaps from afar – or even autonomously. A general example is how knowledge of electromagnetism enables us to observe brain function, store information, communicate instantaneously across the planet and into space, travel at high speeds, light and heat our homes – magnetism underlies fMRI scanners, maglev trains, video tapes, laptop hard drives, earphones, microphones, and much more. As this shows, technological development branches and proliferates as well as accelerates and creates.

I labour these points because they are relevant to the reasons why international cooperation is needed in relation to technology, for though many present and forthcoming kinds of technology offer boons to humanity, other kinds threaten dangerous and undesirable possibilities – in too many cases, extremely dangerous and highly undesirable. Their spread and development, and what further developments they suggest, are causes of grave concern. In light of the self-interest Law, the most that might be feasible in relation to them is restraint and management or at very least delay, which gives time for the development of countermeasures. Though the Law alas suggests pessimism about achieving the ideal, which is outright prevention of the most dangerous versions of these technologies, that is no reason not to try for it. It is most certainly still relevant to warn.

In this arena it matters that the positive promises of technology be kept in mind because, if they are not, focus on both legitimate and fanciful fears can lead to a blanket Luddism. This would be as unhelpful as ignoring negative possibilities. Moreover, the second part of the self-interest Law has to be broken in the case of technologies that are positive for, say, health, education, poverty reduction, and the like, which nevertheless impose loss or cost on some actors in the relevant spheres who have the power to stop or interfere with them, as exemplified by the climate change crisis where deniers and distractors are motivated by the need to protect their own interests – which invariably means their investments and income.

There are many examples of positive technological developments, such as diagnostic tools in medicine, precise microsurgery employing artificial intelligence, interactive education programmes teaching maths to children, and robotics, with robots cutting costs and increasing efficiency in industry and transport – and also, very differently, providing care and companionship for the elderly, thus illustrating the range of possibilities that robotics with AI offer.

There are also many examples of technological developments that have both positive and negative aspects. They include platforms that use communications technology to keep friends and family in touch with each other; provide information of every kind; entertain; store easily retrievable text, audio, and video material; and more. But – all too familiarly – they are also used to spread misinformation, malice, and malware, and for surveillance and invasion of privacy, by some of these means posing threats to democracy.[2] Among the troubling aspects of AI is its use to make decisions on matters that affect people, from assessment of insurance premiums to judicial determinations in court; even when AI is likely to produce consistent, dispassionate, data-based outcomes, the less predictable emotion-influenced decisions made by human beings are – at least in this transitional period of AI adoption – strongly preferred by most people.

Although it is hard to find downsides to some technological developments – how can one dislike the idea of extremely precise brain surgery, or effective and fun on-screen maths lessons? – there can still be costs attached to positive developments. Consider driverless cars. There are huge advantages in these. They will be safer, cheaper, and cleaner than conventional cars. A city that has a large fleet of driverless taxis will benefit hugely: they will obviate the need for private car use within the city because the taxis will be inexpensive, convenient, green, and space-saving, and they will improve the aesthetics of the cityscape. They will be safe because sensors and satellite imaging, automatically moderated speed, distance-keeping, and precise handling mean that other vehicles, cyclists, and pedestrians will be far better protected than now. They will be inexpensive because there will be no drivers to pay, insurance premiums will be lower, as will maintenance costs because of more consistent and moderate operation, and they will be able to operate twenty-four hours a day except for recharging periods. They will be clean because electric, convenient because quick and easy to summon, accurate in their navigation, and expeditious because there will be no or few traffic jams. They will be space-saving because parking lots, garages, and street-side parking will be unnecessary. And they will have a positive effect on the urban environment because street furniture will be redundant – stop signs, traffic lights, direction boards, most of the ugly tangle of posts and signs that disfigure the cityscape, will go; driverless vehicles will find their way and interact with each other by satellite.

The downside is the impact on conventional car sales and maintenance, taxi driver careers, parking lot owners and attendants, oil company profits, and local government revenues from parking charges and tickets. These latter could be discounted if the taxi fleet operator is the local government itself. The other losses do not seem so momentous. But think now of driverless trucks transporting goods around the country. It is already commonplace for large warehouses to be fully automated, requiring no interior lighting and minimal air-conditioning (at below-human-comfort temperatures) because people do not work there except for occasional maintenance visits. Loading trucks at these depots is also automated; unloading at the other end of a supply run can be made so too.

As with driverless taxis, costs are kept down because there are no drivers to pay and the trucks are able to move non-stop other than for charging, loading, and unloading. Insurance will be lower too because of greater safety, and maintenance costs likewise because, again, of more consistent and moderate operation.

Here, however, more downsides appear, because haulage is a large industry providing commensurately high numbers of jobs. In the United States it employs millions of people directly and indirectly – two million directly as drivers, mechanics, dispatchers, clerks, managers, and accountants, and many others indirectly, from gas station attendants to service staff in roadside cafés, from highway maintenance teams to state and local government infrastructure planners. Driverless operation of any kind of vehicle is likely to reduce the costs of road maintenance too, with correlative reductions in the revenues of companies that supply asphalt, concrete, aggregates, and labour.

The downsides here are obviously manageable, though as often happens in a changing or declining industry older personnel can be hard hit. But as automation sweeps across economies, not just in the factory and on the highway but into offices, doctors' surgeries, and schools, questions arise about a major shift in employment – or into unemployment – for large numbers of people. Consider: in 1870 three-quarters of Americans worked in agriculture; by the Second World War the proportion was less than 10 per cent. Because the US economy was growing so feverishly in that period, the shift from agriculture to industry and commerce was painless (except for the negative effects for people migrating from farms to towns and cities). But whereas in 1870 there were twenty-five million horses in the US, by the 1950s there were fewer than seven million. The question to be asked as automation and AI become ubiquitous in our lives and economies is: is our fate that of the horses?[3]

Some argue that, as has normally happened in the past, loss of old industries and jobs will be accompanied or followed by the creation of new industries and jobs. On this view, those displaced from declining or technology-adopting sectors will be absorbed into newly emerging sectors. Either wholly new sectors and opportunities will be created by technology itself, or a ladder effect will apply, in which automation replaces jobs at the bottom of the ladder and adds new jobs at the top.

This latter view is in line with the distinction drawn by the authors of a 2016 OECD report between 'tasks' and 'jobs'; they argue that whereas many *tasks* will be taken over by machines, the fact that there is more to the *jobs* involved – not least in respect of the fact that there are legal and ethical factors implicated in the jobs in question – means that automation is unlikely to displace more than 10 per cent of current jobs. This is a considerably more optimistic assessment than was arrived at by researchers at Oxford University's Martin School, who calculated that 47 per cent of occupations in the US are vulnerable to replacement by automation.[4] Even if one grants that the OECD prognostication is more likely than the Martin School one, a 10 per cent displacement of the workforce would constitute a major event and, at very least in the transition, a turbulent one. Yet on the present horizon of affairs the OECD view seems over-optimistic. This is because the areas of new opportunity likely to emerge from a more automated and technology-driven world will almost certainly require the very aptitudes and skills that reduced the need for human workers in the first place, and which are not widely shared in the populace – namely, aptness for mathematics and coding. Moreover, the automation of more and more kinds of work is far more likely than the creation of non-automatable new kinds of work. The father-and-son team of Richard and Daniel Susskind wrote, in their study of the future of *expert* work which on the face of it seems least vulnerable to automation, that 'Increasingly capable machines, we conclude, will gradually take on more and more non-routine tasks; and so the intuition that there will always be tasks left that only humans can perform will prove to be ill-founded.'[5]

Others argue that in order to cope with a more automated, less person-involving economy, such initiatives as work-sharing, short working weeks, and early retirement will have to be implemented, or – more adventurously – a switch made to a programme in which a universal basic income is combined with opportunities for continuing education and involvement in voluntary work, cultural activities, and hobbies. What palette of solutions is adopted – some or all of the foregoing among them – will depend, obviously, on the degree to which automation displaces human beings in the workplace; the assumption has to be that it will be considerable.

Trying to guess what a more automated economy will look like faces the problem that we think in contemporary terms about norms and expectations. We take the world as it is, then remove the jobs and try to work out what we might do instead, everything else staying the same. This is what leaves space for the optimists who say that something will turn up, and the pessimists who are appalled by the idea of merely filling up time by returning to education and finding a hobby. The latter might ask: what is a life worth that has in it no prospect of growth, achievement, ascent in income and status? The answer might be that learning new languages, increasing one's knowledge in some field, painting, or making furniture, have progression, achievement, and significant rewards built in. If objective benchmarks of success in life include others' admiration or respect, there are as many opportunities in these avocations as in business or politics. A debate of this kind is characteristic of a transitional period in human affairs, when previous norms are dissolving and experiments in new norms are at a hypothetical stage.

The same considerations apply here as to climate change: one should target efforts at the plausible worst-case scenario, to achieve prevention or mitigation of ill-effects, and in this case to prepare to take advantage of potential benefits. Even in a utopian situation where, because of higher productivity and lower costs, automation generates greater wealth than a human-based workforce does, the question of distribution of that wealth becomes crucial, to avoid the evils of too great inequality and most of all a situation where a machine-economy immiserates large swathes of the population with nothing to compensate for their marginalization. There are historical situations which provide clues to how things can go wrong in this respect. A highly automated economy is like a slave-based economy, with very low-cost labour – the costs in effect being basic maintenance; in the case of slaves, subsistence – and for non-slave members of the society who nevertheless are not skilled enough to do, or do not have the opportunity to do, anything apart from the work already done by slaves or machines (or their near-analogues in very cheap labour economies), their otiosity is a toxin both to them and the society at large. Consider 'poor whites' in racially segregated settings like apartheid South Africa and the southern US states between the 1860s and 1960s; had they been a more significant percentage of the population, such as might be the case in a large-scale shift to automation across a developed economy, the social stresses would have been much more serious than they were.

In short, if a large-scale shift to automation simply left 10, 20, 30 per cent of the working-age population with no jobs and no alternatives, matters would be fraught. That is the 'prevent, miti-gate, or at least prepare' scenario to be thought about.

There are yet further aspects of life in which AI and robotics in particular might have a surprising and potentially significant impact. If radical changes in the patterns of work and life implied by the foregoing will alter human relationships, so too will care robots and sex robots.

People have a strong tendency to anthropomorphize inani-mate things even if they do not look like humans or familiar animals. But anything *facially resembling* a human being, such as a doll and the kinds of animal with which humans have long associated, principally dogs and cats, will be endowed with personality and stimulate attachment. Faces or face shapes with big eyes and a small chin, as one typically sees in dolls and cartoon characters, evoke positive responses. The human brain is wired to endow even the simplest representation of what might be a face – the 'emoticons' :) and :(are instantly recogniz-able as happy and sad faces respectively – so the practically featureless round heads on the diminutive care robots ('care-bots') used as assistants and companions to elderly and disabled folk in Japan still prompt affection and dependency in the latter.[6]

Care and affection given by human beings to elderly folk would obviously be much better than care and assistance by robots. But when human carers, or human kindness, are in short supply, a care robot is a very good substitute – vastly better than nothing. The more sophisticated their AI and mechanical capa-bilities, the better. But as current care robots show – including therapeutic robots such as Paro – they do not have to be completely lifelike to be effective. Paro is a fluffy, cuddly, white seal doll, with advanced interactive capabilities, somewhat impressionistic as a representation of a baby seal but effective, especially with dementia patients.[7] Therapeutic robots have similar effects on people as pet animals do, lowering blood pressure and stress levels, and providing a sense of companionship.

Lifelikeness is not essential to carebots, but it is a chief aim of the sex robot (sexbot) industry, and here there is much more controversy.

Sex dolls have a long ancestry, doubtless stretching back way before the masturbation dolls made for sailors on long voyages centuries ago. It was inevitable that robotics, materials science, and AI would transform the sex doll into the sex robot, and development in the relevant technologies proceeds apace. Most of them take the form of nubile young women; one producer of them, Realrobotix, can provide bespoke versions of its 'Harmony' sex robot, varying bust size, hair, voice, and even character, according to customer preferences.[8] Matters have come a long way since the inflatable sex doll beloved of comedy shows. Male-form sex robots are also produced, but the demand for them is insignificant in comparison to female-form versions.

Critics of sex robots say that sex should be part of fully human relationships which valorize intimacy, mutual concern, and affection, and that the availability of sex robots will diminish their occurrence, desensitizing people to intimacy and empathy and promoting social isolation.[9] They regard sex with sex robots as unhealthy and unnatural. They point to the complete objectification involved, reinforcing the view of women as mere devices to be used for sexual gratification. Very serious concerns arise over sex robots programmed for rape scenarios and sex robots in the form of children; by providing opportunities for rapists and paedophiles to act out their desires, the critics say, commission of such acts in reality will become more likely.[10] One result of the debate has been formation of the Campaign Against Sex Robots, seeking to outlaw them altogether.[11]

Defenders of sex robots point out that there are many lonely men who cannot find sexual partners, that sex robots are a boon to disabled individuals,[12] and even that aberrant or dangerous proclivities can be contained by providing robot outlets for them – this last is argued by Shin Tagaki, a confessed paedophile sex robot manufacturer.[13] Despite the claim that women might find a well-endowed and high-performance male-form sex robot of interest, not least because it can be switched off and locked in the cupboard afterwards, 'no mess, arguments, cooking, washing socks involved', there is relatively little interest in that quarter, the argument being that women are more interested in the emotional than just the physical aspects of sexual relations.[14]

The case of sex robots illustrates the kind of dilemma that technology represents, bringing advantages to some, anxieties to others; solving problems for some, yet bringing problems in their wake. Recall the self-interest Law: 'What can be done will be done if it brings advantage or profit to those who can do it' despite efforts to stop it: this makes it inevitable that sexbot technology will be developed, and that both benefits and harms will occur as predicted. But it also illustrates how the situation can be managed through rational policy, the benefits being allowed and the harms minimized. This is a case where regulation is better than proscription.

Claims that sex 'should' be restricted only to a certain promoted form of interpersonal relationship are debatable. The assertion that robots will promote isolation and insensitivity is questionable – both exist without their help already. It is certainly right that rape-scenario and child-form sex robots should be banned outright, and they already are in some countries.[15] But the policy of shooting all dogs because some of them bite is clearly disproportionate. Neither blanket permission nor blanket prohibition is the right way forward. The former is not desirable, given the negatives; the latter is unwarranted, goes too far, and will anyway be ineffective. But there is a clear case for legal intervention in the cases described, as there is for controlling assault rifles, making driving over an alcohol limit illegal, and other such efforts at harm prevention and containment.

Questions about what will happen in the worlds of work and interpersonal relationships are specific. They are part of more general questions that arise in the two arenas of artificial intelligence and social media, some of the connections between them troubling, some of the applications and potentials of each even more so. Here there is much to discuss, because machine learning, robotics, and nanotechnology raise serious questions about weapons and weapons systems, surveillance and privacy invasion, hacking, spying, data mining and fraud, manipulation of social and democratic processes, and neuropsychological interventions.

Privacy loss, hacking, spying, and fraud are major downsides of the new technologies, which have hugely potentiated all four. These are problems we already face, right now in the present, and they are familiar. Here I focus on the hazards implicit in three other areas related to these. One is certain other facets of AI itself; the second is autonomous weapons; the third is aspects of neuropsychological interventions which amount, in reality, not science fiction, to mood manipulation, mind reading, and control. These too are all present in the world today, but less familiar.

And finally, attention needs to be paid to the dangers posed by social media platforms in social and political arenas, in ways that are already doing much harm.

International agreement restraining development and deployment of autonomous weapons systems is urgent and the need for it obvious. These weapons systems exist already, and hundreds of billions of dollars are devoted annually to their ongoing development. The question whether international cooperation is needed on the other two matters – to combat political misuse of social media and less benign interventions in neuropsychology – might seem less obvious, but indeed it is so. Interference by one country in another's elections using social media (and hacking) has already taken place – Russia's involvement in the United States presidential elections of 2016 and 2020 has been well documented and the subject of Congressional enquiry.[16] Nanotechnology and research into 'BCHIs' – 'brain-chip interfaces' – are advancing hand in hand.[17] Here such benefits as controlling epilepsy, combatting Parkinson's disease, repairing the deficits caused by strokes, enhancing memory, restoring vision, and more, make the prospect of intervening in the brain in this way highly attractive. But the anxiety is that the same technology – perhaps the very same devices – can have malign applications also.

Consider AI first.[18] People in developed countries are used to the fact, even if they are only vaguely aware of it, that almost everything in their lives is run by computer. Their energy and water supplies, their communication and other devices, the banking system they use, the delivery of provisions to their local supermarket, the aeroplanes and cars they travel in, the factories that produce the goods they buy, the security systems that police their society – things constituting the very framework of ordinary life – depend upon computers. Computers are not, by themselves, AI devices; they deterministically execute algorithms that have been programmed into them. As the name implies, 'artificial intelligence' denotes a capacity to replicate human cognitive abilities, behaving intelligently in the sense of solving problems, making connections, storing and applying memories, adapting in response to patterns in input data. AI 'brings computers into life and turns them into something else'.[19] For those in whose minds these words evoke Hal of *2001: A Space Odyssey* and *The Terminator*, the idea of 'bringing computers to life' and 'turning them into something else' sets off alarm bells. James Barratt reports that many experts engaged in AI development are confident that 'in the future all important decisions governing the lives of humans will be made by machines or humans whose intelligence is augmented by machines'. But almost all those he interviewed were also confident that the resulting dispensation will be benign, and transition to it painless and incremental.[20]

And then the thought, the prospect, of artificial intelligence greater than human intelligence – *superintelligence* – comes immediately to mind. In line with the view just expressed about the benign character of AI, governance by superintelligence has a utopian ring – would not such a world be rational, just, supremely well-organized? – until one recalls that the current world is believed by people with a religious outlook to have a superintelligent governor already, and the best version of their theodicy – the explanation of why a God-governed world is nevertheless full of suffering and evil, theodicy being the 'justification of the ways of God to man' as Milton put it – is that a perfect world would not be the best of all possible worlds, and therefore suffering and evil are part of the divine superintelligence's plan.[21] Might superintelligent AI systems think likewise? Indeed, a wholly logical and emotionless superintelligence might ask itself what is the most disruptive and destructive thing on the planet, correctly identify human beings as this thing, and proceed to exterminate them therefore; and this would be a rational choice on utilitarian grounds, weighing the interests of all the plant and animal species on the planet against the interests of humans.[22] A superintelligence need only be intelligent enough to make that calculation, and powerful enough to act on it.

Matters might be yet worse. Barratt writes:

> The smooth transition to computer hegemony would proceed unremarkably and perhaps safely if it were not for one thing: intelligence. Intelligence isn't predictable just *some* of the time, or in special cases ... computer systems advanced enough to act with human-level intelligence will likely be unpredictable and inscrutable *all of the time*. We won't know at a deep level what self-aware systems will do or how they will do it. That inscrutability will combine with the kinds of accidents that arise from complexity, and from novel events that are unique to intelligence.[23]

The classic discussion of anxieties about superintelligent AI is provided by the philosopher Nick Bostrom in his *Superintelligence: Paths, Dangers, Strategies*. 'If some day we build machine brains that surpass human brains in general intelligence, then this new superintelligence could become very powerful. And, as the fate of the gorillas now depends more on us humans than on gorillas themselves, so the fate of our species would depend on the actions of the machine superintelligence.'[24] The problem that confronts us, therefore, is the 'control problem', namely, how we ensure that the superintelligence that emerges from AI developments will 'protect human values'. For the kind of reason Barratt identifies – the creative and unpredictable aspect of intelligence – this, Bostrom remarks (in something of an understatement), 'looks quite difficult. It also looks like we will only get one chance. Once unfriendly superintelligence exists, it would prevent us from replacing it or changing its preferences. Our fate would be sealed.'[25]

There are two terms in the foregoing discussion of anxieties, one used by Barratt and one by Bostrom, that are important for this discussion. Barratt speaks of 'self-awareness' on the part of a superintelligence; Bostrom uses the phrase 'general intelligence'. This latter is the key notion in more apocalyptic anxieties about AI, *artificial general intelligence* being what properly mimics human intelligence and which, when it comes to transcend human intelligence, could pose the risks identified. All AI as it exists at time of writing replicates the cognitive functionality of bees, owls, cows, and creatures of that kind – that is, creatures generally speaking possessed of less cognitive capacity than non-human primates and dogs, scarcely meriting the term 'intelligence' – if this by definition includes, as it must, adaptive and creative aspects – because its operation is targeted to, and limited to, a particular task or range of tasks, its competence not extending beyond what is required for executing them. Relative to these programmed kinds of task, AI regularly far outstrips human capacity already; it can beat world champions at chess and Go; it can perform with extreme rapidity huge mathematical computations that would take teams of human mathematicians many lifetimes; it can be accurate, precise, unvaryingly consistent and efficient in carrying out such functions as spot-welding, facial recognition, medical diagnostics, and identification of patterns in enormous data sets. These are all *specific* tasks. Much of the AI already in operation is very smart in these ways. But although there are ethical problems and worries about these specific sorts of AI – discussed later – the major worry is artificial *general* intelligence, 'AGI'.

The question of self-awareness is most likely to arise in connection with AGI, and although it would not be necessary for AGI to be self-aware for it to calculate that, for example, planet earth would be better off without humans on it, it might be necessary for more nuanced kinds of judgment in which utilitarian considerations of this kind fail to persuade – perhaps because there are goods whose preservation outweighs a basic utility trade-off; for example, those for which a degree of environmental damage is a cost worth paying, such as (say) the productions of artistic genius. In weighing interests, affective and subjective dimensions have a claim, and indeed it might be that these are greatly more important than purely quantifiable ones. An AGI might therefore have to be self-aware and capable of appreciating – perhaps indeed of experiencing – these qualitative properties in order to judge whether, for example, human beings should be exterminated to save the current version of planet earth's ecology.

The 'control problem' identified by Bostrom arises in connection with AI and especially AGI coming to transcend human ability to direct it, understand it, and constrain it if it begins to behave in human-threatening ways. AI already teaches and develops itself – the unsupervised and reinforcement models of *deep learning* (machine learning effected by multiply-layered neural networks enabling a system to teach itself without direction) are now standard as a way of furthering AI capacities; DeepMind's AlphaGo system, for example, taught itself to play the game. And the thought is that when a system designs itself to be smarter and then smarter again, continually enhancing its capacities in ever-shortening time scales, matters could get out of hand. The possibility of this happening was envisioned as long ago as 1965 by I. J. Good (Isadore Gudak), who described as 'an intelligence explosion' what would happen if an intelligent system came to understand its own design and enhanced itself again and again in a feedback cycle.[26] The potential for such a system to continue getting ever more intelligent thereafter is open-ended. A name is given to the moment when an AGI system will outstrip human intelligence: 'the Singularity'. Given the creativity, novelty, and unpredictability of intelligence – these characteristics being part of its definition – when the Singularity occurs, it would seem – as Bostrom indicates – that all bets are off.[27]

As noted above, anxieties about the potential dangers of superintelligent AGI are dismissed or downplayed by those who think either that it will never happen, or that it is very unlikely to happen in the foreseeable future; and they correlatively point out – quite rightly – the many benefits that AI brings and will bring. They argue that critics focus too much on what AI might take away – jobs, decision-making in some spheres, autonomy in other spheres – and too little on what it offers: 'different and better jobs, new conveniences, freedom from drudgery, safer workplaces, better health care, fewer language barriers, new tools for learning and decision-making that will help us all be smarter, better people'.[28]

Grant that it is an open question whether superintelligent AGI will happen, and if so when. Nevertheless, and granting too all the positives that the optimists list, the rational course is to decide how to prepare for superintelligent AGI if it does happen. That means trying to anticipate the forms it could take, and it means considering worst-case scenarios and having a plan for how to deal with them, if possible. Some of what needs to be said about AI – the AI already in operation in so much of what happens in the world – and the likely enhancements in capacities of current AI programmes specific to given domains of activity such as air traffic control and trading on stock markets, will apply to AGI too. But the questions specific to AGI, especially if it were to turn out to be 'unfriendly', are close in kind to questions about what we think about dictators, tyrants, and human rights violators. It is not *what* might exercise such dominion, but *why* we do not want anything to exercise such dominion, most especially an intelligent such thing given that its intelligence could negate our efforts against it.[29]

What we want in respect of the AI systems already operating is that they be transparent to inspection, predictable in their operation, and robust against hacking and manipulation.[30] This is especially so for AI systems whose outputs have social dimensions such as determining whether an individual is creditworthy and can be advanced a loan, has a behavioural history that influences whether she can be offered a job or granted parole from a prison sentence, has a sufficiently good prognosis to merit extension of medical insurance coverage, and the like. Already AI is making actuarial decisions about life insurance premiums; Bostrom and Yudkowsky imagine a situation in which an algorithm for evaluating mortgage applications systematically rejects those made by members of a particular race. This is uncomfortably closer to reality than one would like; an investigation by ProPublica showed that black defendants in criminal cases were sentenced at twice the rate of white defendants for comparable offences.[31] This shows that it is essential that AI systems be open to inspection to find out why bias is occurring if it manifests in outputs. Some systems, such as those based on complex neural networks, may never be transparent. Others, such as those based on Bayesian networks, can be investigated. To guard against injustice, accordingly, socially impacting systems have to be based on something more like the latter; they have to be scrutable.[32] They also have to be predictable; outputs that do not manifest a consistent pattern undermine the stability that a social environment requires. And they also have to be secure; systems that monitor airline passengers to detect anyone carrying a bomb or firearm must be safe from hacking.[33]

The acceptability of AI systems whose outputs have social dimensions turns crucially on accountability. When things go wrong, it must be possible to identify who takes responsibility – whether the owners, operators, or designers of the system. It is common enough practice for bureaucrats to hide behind the shield of widely dispersed shared responsibility, making it complicated for anyone seeking a remedy for harms done to them by a bureaucracy, but we nevertheless expect accountability to lie somewhere. The same has to apply to socially impacting AI systems.[34]

And clearly, these systems have to be controllable; if they malfunction or get out of hand, we need to have some way to stop them.

An obvious problem with superintelligent AGI is that these requirements and expectations, and in particular the last one mentioned, might be unfulfillable. This repeats Bostrom's point that the chief problem is the 'control problem'. How are the potential risks of 'unfriendly superintelligent AGI' to be prevented or at least managed? In 2015 an open letter, signed by Stephen Hawking, Elon Musk, Oren Etzioni, and Max Tegmark, among others, was circulated publicly calling for attention to be paid to the safety of AI.[35] While recognizing the benefits of AI, the signatories insisted on the need for humans to remain in charge of it to ensure that it will be beneficial and safe. In a paper written in association with the open letter, four desiderata are identified:

> *Verification:* How to prove that a system satisfies certain desired formal properties. (Did I build the system right?) *Validity:* How to ensure that a system that meets its formal requirements does not have unwanted behaviors and consequences. (Did I build the right system?) *Security:* How to prevent intentional manipulation by

unauthorized parties. *Control:* How to enable meaningful human control over an AI system after it begins to operate. (OK, I built the system wrong; can I fix it?)[36]

The open letter, the associated paper, and the concluding chapter of Bostrom's book speak only in general terms about how to confront the worst-case risks of superintelligent AGI. The most definite proposal is that those working in AI restrain themselves from working towards or allowing its development. For one thing, the self-interest Law makes that a forlorn hope; for another, *ex hypothesi* superintelligent AGI might emerge from a deep learning process without human intention. The transition moment from AI – narrow AI, targeted on one function such as facial recognition or air traffic control – to superintelligent AGI might occur unpredictably. For this reason some wish to outlaw any developments that might lead to it. Once again, the self-interest Law considerations militate against the efficacy of such a strategy, even if it were desirable, and arguably it is not, because it would place constraints on the continued development of good AI with important benefits for humanity. Almost everyone would, however, wish to see AI development occurring in such a way that, if or when it escapes human control, it *always* steers itself in alignment with human values and interests – that the very DNA of AI, so to speak, incorporates this. The problem here is that trying to bake-in an instruction that the system cannot override, such as 'never do anything that harms humans', stands in contradiction to what the system autonomously creates itself to be, which precisely is – among other things – *autonomous.* We try to steer our children, when they are growing up, towards being socially cooperative and beneficent, yet for all the education and conditioning we attempt, quite a few do not turn out as we wish. (Which is, in some respects, actually a good

71

thing, in relation to humans at least; society would become too sclerotic, conventional, and conservative otherwise.) Given that an AGI's 'upbringing' by deep learning already lies – by definition – outside any human programming, the hope that it will teach itself good manners and tenderness towards humanity is not a well-grounded one.

This therefore leaves open the question, still being debated and still to be resolved, about what we – we human beings; humanity – should do about the possibility of unfriendly superintelligent AGI. Superintelligent AGI might never happen; it might happen but be friendly; it might happen, its happening might be inevitable, it might already be on the way or even here, and it might *already* be the case that there is nothing humans can do about it. But as with the climate problem, doing nothing, trying nothing, not thinking, not seeking to prevent a disaster, or to mitigate or prepare for it, is not an option. The effort transcends national boundaries because it is not a local but a global issue.

Suppose the arrival of very unfriendly superintelligent AGI were known to be imminent – say, in a year's time, and that the processes from which it is emerging are themselves unstoppable. Could a countermeasure AI system be built, or a trip switch cutting off all forms of energy generation worldwide that the malign AGI would draw upon – and so on for increasingly fanciful ideas: but desperation would be the mother of invention here. Would any countermeasure be possible, at that scale and in that time frame, unless it were global? The analogy that comes to mind is a global pandemic disease such as Covid-19 and the effort to develop and distribute vaccines. The lesson it teaches is clear.

A final and little-discussed arena of difficulty regarding superintelligent AGI concerns whether we would have ethical responsibilities towards it. This is acutely so if AGI achieves self-awareness, which means consciousness of its own existence and at least some of what this implies – namely, having purposes and interests, and thus in effect being a *person*. The concept of a person is a forensic concept in ethics and law, relating to the kind of thing that has responsibilities and rights – so a corporation is a person in law, whereas a newborn infant or someone suffering dementia is strictly speaking not a person, though of course as human beings they are or should be accorded all the *rights* of personhood (not the responsibilities) given the interest we have in caring for our kind.

There are complexities here. Let us introduce a distinction between a *moral agent* and a *moral patient*, defining the first as something that has moral responsibilities, the second as something worthy of moral regard. Thus, a chicken is not a moral agent, but it is a moral patient for at very least the reason that it can suffer fear and pain and this fact places a constraint on how we should treat it if, as we do, we regard infliction of uninvited and especially unwelcome fear and pain on any sentient being as a wrong. The paradigm case of a being which is both a moral agent and a moral patient is any normal adult human being. The question now is: what has to be true of a superintelligent AGI for it to be both an agent and a patient in the moral sense, and are there any circumstances in which it is just one of these things – only an agent, say? – so that switching it off (killing it) would not be a morally troubling act?

Possession of an independent ability to choose, decide, act, and resist efforts to make it act differently, are implicated in the idea of something's being an agent. It is hard to conceive of agency without self-awareness – 'true' agency, one might say; a wolf acts, but driven by its hunger and hunter's instincts; we do not imagine that it could decide to ignore its hunger and instinct to pursue the rabbit it had seen, in order to contemplate the scenery instead. If a superintelligent AGI had the independent capacity to choose, decide, act, and resist efforts to make it act differently, it would count as a 'true' agent. Differently, possession of self-awareness might be sufficient for a superintelligent AGI to count as a moral patient, given that things (like chickens) without self-awareness already qualify as such. It is conceivable that an AI system might have self-awareness without agency; it would then be in the same position as a chicken, morally speaking. Given that millions of chickens are unceremoniously slaughtered every day, switching off the power supply to a self-aware AI system would be no more troubling than the fate of chickens (at least as far as most people are concerned). This might even be so if it were thought that in addition to self-awareness such a system were *sentient* – not just able to register on its instruments facts about its environment such as the temperature or strength of the wind, but could have sensory experience of both – could *feel* them. A chicken can feel the temperature and the breeze, but still does not command enough moral regard by most people to save itself from factory farming and the standard forms of butchery used in slaughterhouses.

From this assembly of considerations it would be safe to say that if a superintelligent AGI has agency and is self-aware, and even more so if it is sentient, it is a person, and has full moral status equivalent to a human person. It is even arguably the case that if it were self-aware and possessed agency, but was not sentient, it would still deserve this status. At the minimum, if it is self-aware and no more, it has no less of a claim to moral regard than a chicken. The question of the place in the moral universe of superintelligent AGI, therefore, is not only a matter of what advantages and dangers it might represent to us, but what claims it makes on us in return.

Although the foregoing discussion focuses largely on the question of superintelligent AGI, many and serious ethical questions already cluster around the nature and uses of existing narrow AI. Some of the areas where problems can arise have already been mentioned – job hiring, sentencing and parole, insurance coverage, and more. Take two further examples: AI-mediated communication, in which algorithms operate to optimize achievement of communication goals between people by modifying, enhancing, or supplementing messages; and 'deepfake' technology, in which video images of people can be manipulated to make them appear to say or do things that they did not say or do.

In the first case, problems arise if one cannot be sure how much of an interlocutor's message is a true reflection of what she intended to communicate, whether her message and the intentions behind it can be wholly relied upon if it has been altered or embellished by an AI intervention, or whether indeed the message was entirely generated on someone's behalf by AI.[37] An analogy is provided by the difficulty of judging (say) a university applicant's writing ability if his essay has been modified by a program like Grammarly. There are questions of trust at issue, making AI-mediated communication an instance of a more general concern about whether humans will increasingly be tempted to abdicate responsibility for their utterances and choices by outsourcing them to machines, and hiding behind the machines if ill-consequences follow ('I didn't really mean that, it was the AI . . .').

The potential for malicious applications of 'deepfake' is even more troubling. One of the pioneers of the technology, Supasorn Suwajanakorn, took a hint from long-standing Photoshop technology and used AI and three-dimensional modelling to produce extremely realistic fake videos, synchronized to audio, capable of making people speak and act in ways they never did. Conscious of the potential for misuse, a number of organizations and players in the field (including Suwajanakorn himself) have worked at countermeasures. The AI Foundation's Reality Defender platform offers journalists and campaigners the opportunity to upload videos to be analysed for authenticity.[38] In the arms race undoubtedly in progress, the possibility of extremely damaging deepfakes, from the personal level to the level of global peace, remains.

The general problem with the deep machine-learning technology that underlies AI is that, as noted, the more complex it is the less transparent it is. One can worry about whether biases already present in data are picked up and amplified in the learning process; yet more troubling is the possibility of not understanding exactly what it is the machine has learned, and of being unable to predict or understand the non-human errors that a complex set of algorithms might make. Even in the case of systems which are transparent, monitored, and correctable, the scale of AI functioning can make manipulation or errors catastrophic – in 2010 and again in 2015 error (or perhaps manipulation) in Wall Street trading algorithms threatened trillions of dollars in losses in a stock exchange 'flash crash'.[39] Error anywhere – from examination results to medical diagnoses to automatic activation of weapons systems – could be of the same or greater scale.

Another arena of AI application, raising serious and more immediate concerns because it is already with us, has just been mentioned: namely, weapons of war, and in particular *lethal autonomous weapons systems*, with the chilling acronym LAWS, in which the most troubling word is 'autonomous'.

War has always been a driver of technological development. Indeed, war might well be the driver of civilization itself, over the course of history making greater levels of social organization necessary to muster, equip, train, and organize fighting forces, together with the central authority needed to raise taxes to pay for it all.[40] A prime factor in the ambitions of defence and conquest for which such forces were needed has most often been the balance of superiority in the weaponry deployed.

Recent conflicts in which US and other Western armed forces have taken part, such as those in Iraq and Afghanistan in the first decades of the twenty-first century, showed a new-old kind of soldier, wearing armour once more under his camouflage battle-dress, but highly technologized, wired up, in full communication with comrades and commanders, supplied with night-vision goggles, and carrying weapons of vastly greater power than his predecessors in earlier wars.[41]

Although the crude basis of armed conflict is as it ever was – to destroy or degrade the enemy's capacity and will to fight, at every level from the individual enemy soldier to the economic and political system behind him – war has changed in a number of dramatic respects technologically and therefore in character. This evolution is making war a new kind of phenomenon in significant respects, prompting new and urgent ethical questions.

The reason is the advent of remote unmanned military machines, among them machines that are not merely unmanned but autonomous. Surveillance and hunter-killer drones such as the Predator and the Reaper, used in Afghanistan, the border territories of Pakistan, and Iraq, to 'find, fix and finish' human targets, are already familiar. These devices suggest – perhaps indeed presage – a future of war in which the fighting is done by machines, some of them independently of direct human control. This scenario prompts great anxieties.

Almost all technological advances in weaponry and techniques of warfare bring new ethical problems. The St Petersburg Declaration of 1868 outlawed bullets, then newly invented, that expand and fragment on penetrating a victim's body to increase their incapacitating effect. These 'dum-dum' style bullets are now standardly purchasable in gun shops in the United States.[42] The Hague Convention of 1899 – before heavier-than-air flight had become possible – outlawed aerial bombardment; for example, throwing grenades or dropping bombs from manned balloons and dirigibles. Chemical weapons such as mustard gas were outlawed after the 1914–18 war. Since 1945 attempts have been made to ban or at least limit the spread of nuclear weapons.

These are, however, all examples of futility. The most difficult kind of race to stop or even limit is a weapons race. The development of military technologies is the purest example of the self-interest Law at work. Throughout history technology has been the chief differentiator in war – the spear, the metallurgy of swords and shields, armour, the crossbow, the arquebus, artillery, rapid-fire small arms, aircraft, missiles, the logistical equipment used in moving forces and supplies, all represent the inventiveness prompted by times of urgency, emergency, and danger. Not invariably but generally, whoever has possessed the more advanced military technology has usually had the better chance of winning. Radar, navigation and bomb-aiming devices, developments in the detection of submarines, code decipherment, continual enhancement of the speed and manoeuverability of aircraft, contributed as much to winning the Second World War for the Allied side as the ferocity and sacrifice of Russian troops.

Asymmetric warfare, in which small groups of insurgents can encumber huge military resources of an orthodox kind, directly challenge this trend. Insurgent and guerrilla forces can deny victory to better-equipped forces, though their own prospect of winning has to rely mainly on the long and costly process of attrition, wearing down the willingness of the superior forces to continue. Afghanistan is a prime example; both Russia and the United States exhausted their willingness to prolong the fruitless struggle with guerrilla forces there, fighting whom was like trying to wrestle a fathomless mist.

But the possessors of advanced technology are not wholly without resource. Unmanned drones, used for surveillance and offensive engagement in terrains and circumstances where conventional forces are at a disadvantage, are a prime example. The Afghanistan–Pakistan border 'badlands' provided a classic demonstration of where drones best do their work. Able to stay aloft for long periods, hard to detect and defend against, formidably armed, they are very effective. And they put no operating personnel at risk.

The fact that drones are unmanned, controlled from thousands of miles away by operators sitting safely before a screen doing something reminiscent of playing video war games like 'Call of Duty' and 'Combat Mission', somehow seems to make them more sinister, less 'fair' and right. One is reminded of the world press's reaction in 1911 when the first aerial bombing took place. An Italian airman threw grenades out of his monoplane onto Ottoman troops in North Africa. The world's press were outraged at the 'unsporting' nature of the venture, on the grounds that the victims suffering on the ground were unable to retaliate. This very soon proved wrong; Ottoman troops shot down an Italian airplane the following week, with rifle fire. The moral outrage evaporated fairly quickly; in the following two world wars millions of tons of high explosives were dropped on civilian populations as a matter of course, for years.

Paradoxically, drone activity is at the less bad end, if there can be such a thing, of causing death from the air. It is more selective, more precisely targeted, and therefore marginally less likely to cause collateral damage, than conventional bombing, and as mentioned it keeps one's own out of harm's way: a great attraction for a home team. The seemingly inhuman nature of their operation – the deadly machine without a person in it, faceless, remote, weighed down with missiles, remorselessly homing in on its target – is a prompt for extra dislike of it; yet it reprises a form of killing that anciently recommended itself: like long-range missiles, or high-level carpet bombing, it embodies the same principle as stoning to death, distancing the killer from the victim at a sanitary remove.

Only consider: no RAF bomber pilot in the Second World War would have liked to shoot a woman and her child in the head with a pistol, but on repeated occasions he released huge tonnages of bombs on many faceless women and children in the dark cities below him. Not touching the victim, not being physically nearby, is a sop to the conscience. Screen-gazers in an American desert who steered their drones to targets in Afghanistan have the advantage over bomber pilots of guaranteed safety as well as the stone-thrower's remove.

The history of drones – more technically known as 'unmanned aerial vehicles' (UAVs) – is surprisingly long. They exist to undertake tasks considered 'too dull, dirty or dangerous' for human beings, and in their high-tech current forms perform this role to even greater effect. There were rudimentary UAVs before the First World War, used for target practice; there were flying bombs in the Second World War (the V1 and V2 missiles); there were decoys and surveillance UAVs in the Arab-Israeli Yom Kippur War of 1973; while in Vietnam they undertook over three thousand reconnaissance missions. But after 2001 military UAVs became increasingly significant in US operations in the Middle East and Afghanistan, in both surveillance and hunter-killer roles. The Predator drone became operational in 2005, the Reaper in 2007; since then they have grown in number to constitute almost a third of US aircraft strength, and have been used in many thousands of missions against targets across those regions.

Hunter-killer drones over Afghanistan are remotely operated from bases in the United States, such as Creech Air Force Base near Las Vegas. In the terminology of remote warfare, drones are described as 'human-in-the-loop' weapons, that is, devices controlled by humans who select targets and decide whether to attack them. There are 'human-*on*-the-loop' systems, capable of selecting and attacking targets autonomously, but with human oversight and ability to override them. Examples include the Phalanx CWIS ('sea-wizz') air-defence system used by the US, British, Australian, and Canadian navies, 'capable of autonomously performing its own search, detect, evaluation, track, engage and kill assessment functions',[43] and Israel's Iron Dome system intercepting rockets and shells fired from Palestinian territory. Both Israel and South Korea have automated sentry systems whose heat and motion sensors inform human monitors if they have detected people in their vicinity.

The technology causing most concern, however, is 'human-*out-of*-the-loop' systems, completely autonomous devices operating on land, under the sea, or in the air, programmed to seek, identify, and attack targets without any human oversight after the initial programming and launch.

The more general term used to designate all such systems is 'robotic weapons', and for the third kind 'lethal autonomous robots', 'lethal autonomous weapons systems' (LAWS), or – colloquially and generally – 'killer robots'. There is a widespread view that they could be in standard operational service before the mid-twenty-first century. It is obvious what kind of concerns they raise. The idea of delegating life-and-death decisions to unsupervised armed machines is inconsistent with humanitarian law, given the danger that they would put everyone and everything at risk in their field of operation, including non-combatants. Anticipating the dangers and seeking to pre-empt them by banning LAWS in advance is the urgently preferred option of human rights activists. The 'Campaign to Stop Killer Robots' run by Human Rights Watch has been successful not just in raising public concern but in marshalling support for a ban; at time of writing thirty states, the EU Parliament, the UN Secretary-General, thousands of AI experts and scientists, and nearly two-thirds of people polled on the issue support an outright ban.[44]

International Humanitarian Law already contains provisions that outlaw the deployment of weapons and tactics that could be particularly injurious, especially to non-combatants. LAWS are not mentioned in the founding documents because they did not exist when the documents were first drafted, but the implications and intentions of the appended Agreements and supplementary Conventions are clear enough. They provide that novel weapons systems, or modifications of existing ones, should be examined for their consistency with the tenor of humanitarian law. One of the immediate problems with LAWS is whether they could be programmed to conform to the principle of discrimination, that is, whether they would reliably be able to distinguish between justified military targets and everything else. Could they be programmed to make a fine judgment about whether it is necessary for them to deploy their weapons? If so, could they be programmed to adjust their activity so that it is proportional to the circumstances they find themselves in?

Distinction, necessity, and proportionality are key principles in the humanitarian law of conflict, and in each case flexible, nuanced, experienced judgment is at a premium. Could an AI program instantiate the capacity for such judgment?

An affirmative answer requires AI to be developed to a point where analysis of battlefield situations and decisions about how to respond to them is not merely algorithmic but has the quality of evaluation that, in human beings, turns on affective considerations. What this means is best explained by recalling psychologist Antonio Damasio's argument that if a purely logical individual such as *Star Trek's* Mr Spock really existed, he would be a poor reasoner, because to be a good reasoner one needs an emotional dimension to thought.[45] A machine would need subtle programming to make decisions consistent with humanitarian considerations. Creating a machine analogue of compassion, for example, would be a remarkable achievement; but a capacity for compassion is one of the features that discriminating application of humanitarian principles requires.

Someone might reply to this point by saying that human emotions are just what should *not* be required on the battlefield; machines would be less erratic because never emotionally conflicted; they would be swifter and more decisive in action, and less error-prone, than most if not all humans.

This is true. But the question is whether we wish the decision-maker in a battle zone to be this way, given that among the necessary conditions for conforming to humanitarian law is the capacity to read intentions, disambiguate and interpret odd behaviour, read body language, and the like. These are psychological skills that humans develop early in life, and which they apply in mainly unconscious ways. Would a killer robot be able to tell the difference between a terrified individual trying to

83

surrender and an aggressive individual about to attack? Grasping what a person intends or desires by interpreting her actions is a distinctive human skill. To programme killer robots with such capacities would be yet another remarkable achievement.

What is at issue here is something beyond facial recognition AI, already in existence and already a concern to human rights activists because of surveillance and privacy implications. The 'something beyond' is the capacity of such systems to read and interpret *emotions in faces*. Emotion recognition is offered by Microsoft, Amazon, and IBM as features of their facial recognition software, with obvious benefits to advertisers monitoring responses to their products and marketing campaigns; but it is also claimed that the ability of machines to read emotions has more general applications, from identifying potential terrorist threats to road safety. The risk of deliberate misuse, not least in racial profiling, is obvious; less obvious is the prospect of bad mistakes – for example, someone being shot to death because a system identifies him as an immediate terrorist threat on the basis of what it interprets as his emotional state. According to an expert on the technology, it is already

> in use all over the world, from Europe to the US and China. Taigusys, a company that specializes in emotion recognition systems and whose main office is in Shenzhen, says it has used them in settings ranging from care homes to prisons ... the Indian city of Lucknow is planning to use the technology to spot distress in women as a result of harassment – a move that has met with criticism, including from digital rights organizations.[46]

As this shows, the technology is not merely in development but already in use, and it is inevitable that it will be used in LAWS to identify enemy combatants and read their intentions.

Proponents will once again say that such systems might have a higher degree of reliability in battle situations, where humans are in highly charged emotional states, beset by noise, confusion, and anxiety interfering with their judgment, whereas the dispassionate data-driven algorithm of a LAWS will be more likely to avoid harm to bystanders or to enemy soldiers who have ceased to be a threat.

The answer to this, in turn, is to ask a simple question: if a person smiles, does it invariably and infallibly mean that she is happy? If she smiles, extends a friendly hand, is relaxed in body posture and movements, is this an infallible indicator of her emotional state – and more to the point still: of her intentions? Consider what any actor would say in reply.

Another question concerns who would be held accountable if LAWS went haywire and (say) slaughtered children in an orphanage, demolished hospitals full of sick and wounded, killed everyone it encountered irrespective of who or what they were and what they were doing. Would it be the military's most senior commanders? The programmers? The manufacturers? The government of the state using them? Identifiable accountability is an important feature of humanitarian protection in times of conflict, because the fact of it imposes some restraint on what is done by militaries, and unclarity about it or the absence of it affords too much license.

As noted, agencies such as Human Rights Watch have called for prohibition of the development, manufacture, and use of LAWS internationally and by individual states, and at the same time have advocated adoption by technology firms and laboratories of codes of conduct against research which leads to them. Human Rights Watch quoted a US Air Force document predicting that 'by 2030 machine capabilities will have increased to the point that humans will have become the weakest component in a wide array of systems and processes.'[47] Some years ago – in 2011 – the UK Ministry of Defence estimated that 'fully autonomous systems could be available in 2025'.[48]

At time of writing the governments of countries developing unmanned weapons and robotic systems still officially maintain that they have no intention of allowing their use without human supervision. But one knows what can happen to good intentions. And whereas we know that the advent of LAWS is inevitable, we have no sense of the limits of their further development and future applications – policing demonstrations? Searching for and arresting suspects? Conducting warfare in space? Nanoweapons for assassinations or spreading epidemic disease? The science-fiction imagination, so often anticipating science fact, has no obvious boundaries here.

It could be that systems will be developed that render weapons ineffective – this would be the ultimate stop to war if that were to happen, given that most people would rather make peace than try to kill one another. Is that a pipe dream? In every house connected to an electricity supply there is a trip switch which, when the system overloads or there is a short, turns the power supply off. A trip switch for weapons of every kind would be wonderful. To some extent – so far – the mutual risks of nuclear warfare have constituted, as deterrence, a trip switch against that kind of war; other kinds of trip switches against other kinds of war might yet be possible.

One futuristic form of conflict already entrenched in the present is 'cyberwar'. A preliminary definition, much in need of refinement, was given by Richard Clarke as 'actions by a nation-state to penetrate another nation's computers or networks for the purposes of causing damage or disruption'.[49] The term 'nation-state' needs to be replaced by a more general term to include non-state actors, terrorists not least among them. Thus extended, the term 'cyberwar' encompasses any endeavour to disrupt the computerized systems on which practically all organizations, military and civil, now depend.

In his submissions to the US Senate Armed Services Committee in 2010, General Keith Alexander described cyberwar as the effort to target, and to defend, computer-based military command-and-control systems, communications, weapons systems, and air-defence networks.[50] He could have added that civil networks operating a wide range of facilities from power supply to security and policing arrangements are also obvious targets, as are the operations of many hospitals, research institutions, industries, and commercial enterprises.

One complaint about the term 'cyberwar' is that it fails to capture the many different ways in which penetration of the security of computer systems occurs, and the purposes that attacks on computer security serve. Spying is not the same as sabotage; in the case of efforts to learn the military secrets of a hostile party, sabotaging that party's systems would be self-defeating. Crime and spying between them constitute a problem necessitating massive effort and expense to keep computer systems secure. When it is a case of militaries and their intelligence services trying to penetrate others' military's systems while keeping their own safe, we are close to war as such.

Because of hacking, private sector commercial spying, identity theft, and other such activities, the security of cyberspace is a major issue well beyond the military sphere. But because of the ubiquitous reliance on computing in managing almost every aspect of military activity, cyberwarfare is an inevitable feature of present and future war. And as an alternative to bombing industrial centres, or attacking civilian populations to undermine morale, attacks on the civil systems of modern life to disrupt electricity, water supply, transport, communications, and more, is an obvious and almost certainly far more effective choice.

Even as these words are written there are doubtless researchers developing devices whose role in the future of war we do not yet know or cannot even anticipate. So long as war continues, so long will there be a race to gain technological advantages over real and putative enemies. LAWS, drones the size of mosquitoes, sonic and laser weapons, cyberspace marauders, infiltrators, and saboteurs, violence in space, interdictions of the means of economic and personal life, refined techniques of psychological warfare, indeed approximations of almost anything that science fiction can offer, are almost certainly in current development. The question for the world is whether it is simply going to let this process unfold at its present breakneck speed, with scarcely any effort to limit and control the horrendous consequences that could follow.

The question of AI in weapons systems engages with that aspect of international humanitarian law which concerns *jus in bello*, the actual conduct of armed forces during conflict, leaving aside questions about *jus ad bellum*, which relates to the justifications, if any, there are for going to war in the first place.[51] The rapid evolution of military technology and the nature of conflict has meant that humanitarian law has had to work hard to keep pace – and arguably, has failed to do so, because the evolution of AI and its military applications has been so rapid. The principles of necessity and proportionality are indispensable to a regime of constraint; the intention is to limit the amount of 'collateral damage' that fighting inevitably involves, by requiring that the amount of force used, and indeed whether it is used at all in a given circumstance, should be carefully calibrated to the unintended and unwanted side-effects of its use. The biggest concern about 'killer robots', as with AGI, is their independence of human capacity to restrain them – Bostrom's 'control problem' – and this is a matter of the very definition of the systems in question: recall that LAWS means 'lethal *autonomous* weapons systems'.

The most compelling argument against LAWS can be summed up in three words, constituting a name: Stanislav Yevgrafovich Petrov, who in effect – it does not overstate matters to say so – saved the world single-handedly in 1983. Petrov was a colonel in the Air Defence Force of the Soviet Union who, while on duty at the Oko early-warning facility, chose to disbelieve the system when it showed that half a dozen nuclear missiles had been launched towards Russia from the United States. It should be remembered that this was a notably tense moment in the Cold War; a Soviet fighter plane had shot down a South Korean airliner on 26 September, just three weeks earlier, because the airliner had strayed into Soviet air space and its pilots probably did not see the warning shots fired by the Su-15 interceptor sent up in response to its presence – US spy plane activity was considerable at that time. If Petrov had reported that a missile attack was under way, retaliatory attacks would have been launched, to which the US would have responded in turn, initiating a full-scale nuclear exchange. Petrov decided that the system was malfunctioning, and was proved right. It was possible for a human being to decide to ignore what the system was reporting, on the grounds that a particular constellation of cues suggested as much. Petrov said he was puzzled as to why a US strike would involve so few missiles – surely a serious attack would have been much bigger. Moreover the system was new, and he was not confident that all its bugs had been sorted out. There were many layers of verification for the data to process through, and the system had triggered too quickly for all of them to engage. And finally, ground radar was not seeing what the satellites were reporting. Putting all this together in the extremely short space of time he had to decide, Petrov concluded that no attack was taking place. If the system had been fully autonomous there would – or at least, might quite likely – have been a disaster. An incalculable number of lives were saved by a human being *feeling* that things did not add up.

A sceptic will say that it is more usual for humans to 'feel that things add up' when they do not add up – this being the basis not merely of conspiracy theories but of most ideological commitments. This is no doubt true. But it does not alter the lesson that the Petrov story offers to those who are concerned about the invasion of AI-based automation into arenas, not least the military, where the potential for harm is so very great.

It is a phenomenon of the current age that although there is much debate about the status, promises, and risks of AI and superintelligent AGI, it is also a topic that has surprisingly little traction on the public mind, and efforts to think about the implications and prepare to manage them sensibly are restricted to a relatively small and informed – and in some less helpful cases, obsessed – people whose publications and lectures are the principal source of education and, where appropriate, warning to everyone else. It profoundly matters that there should be a thorough discussion about the management of AI, as the foregoing shows; and it matters that it should be a global discussion, because even if only one government or private agency fosters, permits, or even just ignores the many possible developments and uses of AI as they unfold, the effects will be (as they now are) global anyway. Advertising the most accessible yet authoritative overviews of the need for caution about AI is accordingly

a service, so I do so here: two of the best are provided by Nick
Bostrom and Sam Harris in excellent TED Talks, referenced in
this footnote.[52]

Technological development is not restricted to computing and
AI. Two other arenas where it is raising great hopes for good and
great concern about potential harm are neuroscience and
genetics.

Consider neuroscience first. Already mentioned is the fact
that nanotechnology and research into 'brain-chip interfaces',
'BCHIs', are advancing hand in hand.[53] Here such benefits as
managing epilepsy and Parkinson's disease, dealing with deficits
caused by strokes, enhancing memory, restoring vision and
hearing, communicating with 'locked in' patients, and more, are
on the horizon. Deep brain stimulation is already used to control
Parkinsonism symptoms, and implants aimed at restoring
mobility to victims of paralysis or supplementing or restoring
the senses of sight and hearing are already in development.
These are welcome advances. But it is no longer a science-fiction
possibility that neuroscientific technologies could also be used
in morally questionable ways.

One simple example is 'lie detection'. In the US controversial
use is made of lie detectors, an unreliable and potentially dangerous aid to policing. A new generation of lie detector techniques
based on brain imaging is now mooted as a possibility. At present
neuropsychology does not claim to be able to distinguish
memory, imagination, confabulation, and true and false belief
states on the basis of localizable activations in the brain, but one
observation suggests that if a subject is presented with a description of a memory or putative memory to one hemisphere, a
response is noted in the other hemisphere only if the memory is
genuine.[54] If this is right, an objective measure of the veridicality

of a subject's memories – the details of occurrences at the time a crime was committed would be the case in point here – becomes available.

Likewise the prospect of identifying the *content* of brain states is no longer remote; scanning of visual system activation already provides researchers with indications of what is being seen or visualized.[55] Current developments of this into a capacity to interpret the thoughts of a locked-in patient are a real boon; but extended capacities to do this – perhaps even remotely, say, by scanners located in public places – stands on the current outer edge of both science fiction and moral horror. Yet it is an entailment both of neuroscience's assumptions and its aims that direct communication with brains will be achievable, enabling recognition of the content of cognitive states – in popular parlance: 'mind-reading'. Total loss of the privacy of one's thoughts is one thing, but the implications of fine-grained direct access to brain states goes further than this. It includes the prospect of controlling moods and emotional states, both introducing and changing thoughts and memories, extinguishing existing memories, altering personality, and controlling behaviour, any of these activities with malign as well as benign potential.

For therapeutic purposes, such interventions would be enormously valuable. Alleviating post-traumatic stress, perhaps expunging memories which have a disabling effect on someone's capacity to live normally, would be wonderful for those wishing and willing to find relief in this way. Outside the domain of therapy, and certainly in cases where the subject's consent is not given, such interventions would constitute grave violations of human rights. An ability to generalize these procedures or apply them remotely without the knowledge of those affected is the science-fiction scenario of greatest concern. None of what is

envisaged in these respects lies beyond the bounds of conceiva-
bility given what is already known, and what capabilities already
exist, in neuroscience, and therefore questions about how they
are to be applied and managed need urgent answer.

The list of concerns is long, and its length is itself a prompt to
scepticism about whether any, let alone all, of them are genuine
possibilities. Will brain imaging be accurate and reliable enough
to 'diagnose' criminal personality types and psychopaths before
those so diagnosed behave in socially disruptive ways? PET
(positron emission tomography) scan studies of sentenced
murderers found diminished prefrontal cortex activity, this
region being associated with empathy, self-control, and appre-
ciation of consequences and risks.[56] Could neuroscreening
result in pre-emptive imprisonment, or interventions by pharmacological means or even brain surgery, for those whose
prefrontal cortex activity is below a certain value? A more immediate matter is the use of neurological evaluations in criminal
cases in today's courts, raising difficult questions of culpability
and the right courses of action in sentencing policy.[57]

Other questions are prompted by the idea of neuroscreening.
Will it be possible to infer IQ and aptitudes for different professions from brain scans? What about the detection of unconscious biases and propensities – for racist attitudes, say, or
aggression, depression, and unusual sexual preferences or
hypersexuality? Will prospective employers demand a brain
scan from job applicants to look for trustworthiness, coopera-
tiveness, loyalty, numeracy, sensitivity to stress?

These ideas turn on an implication strongly present in neuroscience: that brain activity, as a natural causal phenomenon, is
deterministic. 'Neurodeterminism' is supported by the kind of
results made famous by Libet and later Haggard and Eimer,
showing that 350 milliseconds before a subject is conscious of a

decision to move a limb, the brain's secondary motor cortex manifests potential readiness to do so.[58] The vexed and familiar problem of free will comes immediately into view, along with a constellation of issues about human nature, autonomy, agency, and the reality of choice on which attributions of criminal and moral responsibility turn. If the findings of Libet and others generalize, it follows that how we standardly think of human beings and human lives is a massive and systematic error.

Leaving these questions aside as relating chiefly to the future – perhaps the near future – there is the already-present question of psychological modification and enhancement of mental powers by direct brain-activity enhancement, using pharmacology and implant technology. The pharmacological story is well known; starting in the Second World War militaries made a practice of providing soldiers and airmen with amphetamine (troops called them 'go-pills' in the 1940s) and caffeine; more recently students have used methylphenidate – a drug used to treat attention deficit disorder – to promote concentration and memory, and modafinil for alertness and reduction of sleep needs before exams. For very much longer than this such substances as alcohol and cocaine have been used to modify moods and overcome shyness, low self-esteem, self-consciousness, and anxiety. The comparison between outlawed performance-enhancing drugs in athletics and intellect-enhancing drugs has prompted some universities to classify use of the latter as cheating.[59]

In comparison to science-fiction prospects of brain implants multiplying a person's cognitive powers many times over, most of the just-mentioned interventions seem crude; even so elementary a procedure as transcranial electrical stimulation is claimed to be more effective and longer-lasting than caffeine in its effects. Moreover, pharmacology carries risks – diminishing efficacy with use, side-effects, overdoses, and confrontations with the law among them. But psychopharmacological neuroscience is progressively refining our knowledge, with more precise understanding of what works, in what ways, and on what structures and substances in the brain, so the pharmacological story is far from over.

Nevertheless, add the attraction of non-drug interventions to combat poor memory, slow apprehension, shyness, depression, and other barriers to educational and social success, and the effort to find technical fixes for underperforming brains is guaranteed: the self-interest Law at work. Moreover, this is a corollary of efforts already long in hand to address a much larger and more immediate problem: repairing damaged brains and damaged psyches. Two examples illustrate how these are now possibilities, not fantasies.

The US Department of Defense's Advanced Research Projects Agency (DARPA) announced its Brain Initiative in 2013, and since then has promoted a wide range of research in collaboration with academic and private agencies. Its website summarizes some of the highly ambitious and far-reaching research in hand:

> The ElectRx program aims to help the human body heal itself through neuromodulation of organ functions using ultraminiaturized devices, approximately the size of individual nerve fibres, which could be delivered through minimally invasive injection... The HAPTIX program aims to create fully implantable, modular and reconfigurable neural-interface microsystems that communicate wirelessly with external modules, such as a prosthesis interface link, to deliver naturalistic sensations to amputees... The Neural Engineering System Design (NESD) program aims to develop an implantable neural interface able to provide unprecedented signal resolution and data-transfer

bandwidth between the brain and the digital world ... the Neuro Function, Activity, Structure and Technology (Neuro-FAST) program seeks to enable unprecedented visualization and decoding of brain activity to better characterize and mitigate threats to the human brain, as well as facilitate development of brain-in-the loop systems to accelerate and improve functional behaviors. The program has developed CLARITY, a revolutionary tissue-preservation method, and builds off recent discoveries in genetics, optical recordings and brain-computer interfaces ... The RAM program aims to develop and test a wireless, fully implantable neural-interface medical device for human clinical use. The device would facilitate the formation of new memories and retrieval of existing ones in individuals who have lost these capacities as a result of traumatic brain injury or neurological disease ... The Revolutionizing Prosthetics program aims to continue increasing functionality of DARPA-developed arm systems to benefit Service members and others who have lost upper limbs. The dexterous hand capabilities developed under the program have already been applied to small robotic systems used to manipulate unexploded ordnance, reducing the risk of limb loss among Soldiers ... The SUBNETS program seeks to create implanted, closed-loop diagnostic and therapeutic systems for treating neuropsychological illnesses ... The TNT program seeks to advance the pace and effectiveness of cognitive skills training through the precise activation of peripheral nerves that can in turn promote and strengthen neuronal connections in the brain. TNT will pursue development of a platform technology to enhance learning of a wide range of cognitive skills, with a goal of reducing the cost and duration of the Defense Department's extensive training regimen, while improving outcomes.[60]

This remarkable programme of research has both a push and a pull component to its motivation. The push comes from the enormous burden suffered by military veterans – and therefore the budget of the Department of Veterans Affairs – of post-traumatic stress disorder in surviving vets from the Vietnam War, the first and especially second Gulf Wars, and the Afghanistan conflict. The psychic injuries caused by exposure to terrifying situations and horrific scenes are the same in any war, but secondary factors have exacerbated the current situation. Prior to the Vietnam War it was common knowledge that only a minority of troops in a conscript army are effective in combat situations.[61] Efforts were made to remedy this in troops sent to Vietnam, by careful psychological preparation. But the war was disliked on the home front and vigorously opposed by vociferous sections of the US population, so returning soldiers did not get the shriving – the indirect rehabilitation effect of social approval – conferred by an environment in which the home community honours military endeavours. In the Gulf and Afghanistan conflicts matters were different; the volunteer soldiers were not only highly trained but a combination of body armour, tactics, and front-line medical treatment ensured that many more of them survived serious injury than would have done so in earlier wars – but with the result that many more of them were disabled, not just physically but in a tsunami of psychological ways. One metric of the problem is the high rate of suicides among returned vets; another is the burden on the Veterans Administration of dealing with the high numbers of cases of spinal cord injury, burns, blindness, amputations, traumatic brain injury, polytrauma, and above all mental illness.[62]

The pull factor is the 'supersoldier' idea, the attempt actually to create cyborg-style warriors whose physical and psychological strengths are augmented by literal neuronal connectedness to supplementary AI. Incredible as it might seem, the model is provided by such notions as Marvel's Captain America and every science-fiction movie from *Robocop* onwards; but if a literal version of the full sci-fi entity takes a while to achieve, superfit and super-efficient soldiers who hardly sleep, suffer no psychological angst, are technologically extremely savvy and well-equipped, and perhaps have their communications and internet connections physically implanted, are not such a remote prospect. The foregoing set of research projects by DARPA are explicit about aiming at nothing less. It is safe to assume that the US is not alone in fostering research in these directions. The director of national intelligence in the US under President Trump, John Ratcliffe, claimed that China is aiming to produce an army of supersoldiers by means of genetic enhance-ment using CRISPR gene editing techniques (on CRISPR see below).[63] Perhaps so; but assuming that the programme began immediately that CRISPR became available in 2012, and assum-ing also that it was rolled out on a massive scale, it would still only be 2030 at the very earliest before the first genetic supersol-diers were ready for action. By that time battalions of DARPA-implanted Marines might already be in service.

The plausibility of all this might easily be questioned, if it were not for Elon Musk's pigs, the star among whom is Gertrude, the brain-chip-wearing porcine demonstrated by Musk in August 2020 during his announcement of progress made by his Neuralink project, and Pager, the macaque monkey whose brain implants enable him to play a video game merely by thinking about hand movements.[64] The avowed aim of Neuralink's research is to find ways of overcoming disabilities caused by brain and spinal cord injuries, which is one reason why the US Food and Drug Administration gave the project Breakthrough Device Designation, at very least thereby signalling a belief in the project's credibility. Because the aimed-for technology involves a brain–machine interface with micrometre-length inserts connecting to neurons, the current state of feasibility prompts scepticism among many in the neuroscientific community.[65]

The rapid expansion of research in neuroscience has brought a new range of ethical concerns into view. In April 2021 the National Academies of Sciences, Engineering, and Medicine in the US published a report examining the implication of research models for study of the human brain involving neural organoids – *in vitro* (that is, in a glass dish) three-dimensional clusters of human brain cells that mimic foetal brains – and the introduction of human brain cells into other animals.[66] When this latter is done at an early stage of an animal's development the result is a chimaera, a part-human hybrid. At time of the report's publication these developments were speculative merely, although experimental introduction of human brain tissue into pig tissue had already been tried, and in the same month of April 2021 researchers at the Salk Institute in California published results in the journal *Cell* of injecting human stem cells into 132 embryos of macaque monkeys.[67] By the twentieth day of the Salk experiment only three embryos remained alive, but the percentage of human cells in them remained high throughout the growth period.[68] The National Academies took the view that some reflection on the ethical dimensions of research like this would be wise; its report concluded that oversight arrangements are (at time of writing) sufficient for managing the creation both of 'mini-brains' and chimaeras, but its authors acknowledged that the pace of developments requires vigilance. This puts matters mildly.

Alongside the many and obvious benefits of developments described in the foregoing, the most serious anxieties concern loss of privacy and autonomy and with them distinctive features of humanness currently valued and protected by regimes of human rights. The dystopian aspects of AI and neuroscience are as easy to imagine as their possible benefits. There seems little to choose between an Orwellian *1984* scenario of tyrannical government surveillance and control in contrast to surveillance and control by business corporations and other private agencies.

One thing the dystopian possibilities suggest is a yet further development, not so far discussed, which brings into the picture troubling possible applications of – this time – genetics: the creation of two versions of humanity, one enhanced and superior, the other a continuation of today's version but subordinate to the others: the arrangement described in Huxley's *Brave New World* (1932). It is an arrangement that has in practice existed in much of the world for much of history in the form of slavery, though if there were any difference between (let alone superiority of) slave-owners to slaves in mental or physical terms it would have been adventitious – a function of nutrition and lifestyle as much as genetics. But gene editing technology introduces a more dramatic and definite possible change, resulting in the production of two versions of the human species – perhaps, indeed, two species of human beings. Application of the self-interest Law to neuroscientific and genetic enhancement of those who can afford it or who will be granted access to it entails that this development is fully on the cards right now. In fact, it has already happened, in the case of biophysicist He Jiankui's use of CRISPR to edit the CCR5 gene in the embryos of twin girls to protect them against the HIV carried by their father.[69]

CRISPR is the acronym for *Clustered Regularly Interspaced Short Palindromic Repeats*. It is a technology for editing genes

– finding a specific piece of DNA in a cell, snipping it out, replacing it with another length of DNA, or simply turning on and off the gene consisting of that DNA. Prior to the discovery of the technique in 2012 there were more laborious and expensive means of doing the same, but this cheap, rapid, and easy method has revolutionized genetic science, and is already widespread in research and development. The potential for good is huge, ranging from creating high-yield strains of insect-resistant food crops to preventing and curing many diseases. In these ways CRISPR offers bright prospects.

The technique was discovered by biochemists Jennifer Doudna and Emmanuelle Charpentier, who were awarded the 2020 Nobel Prize in Medicine as a result. They were studying the proteins used by bacteria to defend against viral infection, 'Cas' proteins, one of which – Cas9 – can readily be programmed to identify and attach itself to any chosen sequence of DNA by giving it a bit of RNA to guide its search. It does this by hunting along the DNA until the target sequence – consisting of twenty letters of DNA (some combination of the four constituent chemical bases adenine, cytosine, guanine, and thymine, abbreviated ACGT) – matches a section of the RNA. By itself this is a remarkable feat, given that the DNA in every cell has six billion letters and is two metres long. When the target sequence is located the Cas9 protein cuts the DNA strand, whose subsequent self-repair introduces mutations that usually result in disabling the gene. This is the main use of the technique; slightly more difficult is modifying the gene; less difficult is switching genes on and off without changing them.

As the case of He Jiankui shows – he was jailed by the Chinese authorities for illegally using CRISPR to modify the genome of human embryos – there are major and obvious concerns about uses of CRISPR which humankind is not yet sure it wishes to make.[70] Jennifer Doudna herself called for a moratorium on CRISPR use in human genome editing until the ethical questions have been properly debated.[71] The questions are principally about what we – 'we' being humanity – would regard as acceptable and desirable in the way of any modification of human beings, and they are also about the dangers of unintended and unpredictable consequences of such changes, even those we regard as beneficent. The obviously desirable changes include making future generations safe not only from heritable diseases but from cancer, cardiovascular disease, Alzheimer's, and other blights on the human frame, however caused. Do we also wish future generations to have higher IQs and more athletic ability? To live for 200 years? To have 'blond hair and blue eyes' as the eugenics fantasy of Nazis desired? This last example dramatizes the problem. For a real-world example of where differences have been made and maintained by what are in effect eugenic practices one might look at the Indian caste system, because whether or not Brahmins are wholly of Aryan descent and Dalits of Dravidian descent, sharp segregation has persisted for over two thousand years.[72]

Someone who favours a Humanity 2 programme of genetic and psychoneurological enhancements might well ask what it is about current humanity, with its tooth decay, heart disease, irrationality, and many other limitations, that we are so keen to preserve. It might also be asked why the values we hold today should constrain future human beings whose outlook on life and the world might be very different from ours. If genetically modified superior humans come into existence, they might regard our values, and indeed our fears and desires, as primitive; we might now be unable to appreciate how things will appear to them, what they want, what will give meaning to their lives, and what uses they will make of future even more advanced technologies in this and other respects.

These are valid considerations. But it will probably be that the self-interest Law will render our haverings over them beside the point. CRISPR exists; and even stringent efforts to outlaw its use in modifying human genomes will be circumvented by those – public or private – in a position to make it happen, which means: in a position to offer enough money to make it happen. Consider the efforts made to outlaw the supply and use of heroin and cocaine; billions of dollars are spent on the effort, to at best modest and usually minimal effect; those who want these substances generally get them. To put the matter another way: if He Jiankui's twins are the only human beings whose genomes have been edited using CRISPR technology at this time of writing, it would be a surprise. Moreover, the question of 'what sort of people should there be?' has long been posed – the philosopher Jonathan Glover published a highly prescient book of that title in 1984; a noteworthy date – and the question it asks has not been answered yet.[73] Indeed the CRISPR revolution is a paradigm of what happens in these domains: humanity fiddles about, usually on the margins, with questions of great and pressing concern, until events gallop past them in a rush so that it is already too late to manage the new situation.

Among the more sinister if currently more speculative possibilities of genetic engineering is its weaponization – for example, the creation of viruses that target only certain populations of people, either whole populations, or just males, or people of military age, or of certain ethnicities; or which target animal or crop food sources most typical of certain geographical regions; or which increase the potency of insects that are vectors for disease in specific regions.

As with the other matters already discussed here, the more

questionable applications of genetic engineering are not something that individual states can hope to manage by acting only within their own borders – assuming that the opportunity for managing them still remains. The question of how to use the technologies of genetic science is a global question for humanity as a whole to answer.

The internet is a prime example of another set of possibilities, many good and many disruptive and potentially destabilizing, brought into existence by technology. Social media, and the ease with which websites can be set up on the World Wide Web, offer universal communication, information sharing, instant news, and a complete democracy of debate and opinion, carrying enormous and transformative promise for a people's world. Beforehand the routes of information and debate were controlled by gatekeepers – editors, publishers, airwaves controlled under license by governments – ensuring a perpetual state of (at very least virtual) censorship, in which only those with appropriate credentials could get a hearing. Blog sites and the advent of social media platforms have broken down the gates that the gatekeepers kept, or almost; they have been re-erected in places like China and Iran, and the abusive and toxic infection of the Web by malign individuals and groups has created so much bad anarchy that the promised good anarchy is under threat. Indeed it is inevitable, as a result, that the honeymoon days of internet freedom are numbered. When they come to an end it is the good anarchy that will suffer most, because bad actors in any field always strive to circumvent limitations, and have a good record of success. In any event the adage 'the bad drives out the good' will apply here as almost everywhere; it is not just coinage that suffers.

One can ignore blogs; the influence of social media is less easy to resist and often scarcely noticed anyway. On the good side, social media connect people and distribute information literally at the speed of light, many positives flowing from both. On the other hand – well: one might begin with the observation that if one is not paying for something, one is not a client but a product. This is the case with Facebook, WhatsApp, Twitter, TikTok, Instagram, email, any facility that one can have 'for free' but for which one is in fact paying with one's data – an enormous amount of data, which is a revenue source for the service providers because they sell it to advertisers and others (the others come into view in a moment) who employ Big Data analytics to profile people and 'microtarget' messaging at them, in the case of advertising companies offering the goods and services that the profile suggests are of interest to people fitting it.

The profiling point is not trivial. Social media providers know more about us than we know ourselves. It can have a more accurate sense of what we like to eat, how we might vote, where we might like to go to next on holiday, than we do. They can choose books, products, fashion items, and entertainment possibilities for us, and they do. When you search for information on Google it will give you the information it thinks you would like to have. Savvy search-engine users make a point of surrounding their searches with wildly random searches in order to throw off the algorithm profiling them.

Having advertising directed at you for beach holidays and cereal products is a benign matter. What immediately springs to mind when profiling and microtargeted messaging are mentioned is the less benign applications of both. Who is Facebook selling your data to? Some version of Cook's Tours is one thing, a political party is another thing, and a government, a police authority, the intelligence service, are different things again. These agencies can have positive uses in mind – the better delivery of health, education, and welfare services; protection of the public against organized crime and terrorism. The potential for *misuse* of such data, perhaps after a change of government or if a more threatening security environment develops, gives pause for thought. Hacking of personal data by criminals is already a widespread problem, but when it is discovered there are at least some prospects of remedy. If information is held on you without your knowledge, some of it perhaps wrong or misleading, and if it is used to make judgments about you, for example, as to whether you can be offered a job or an insurance policy, you are in a very prejudicial situation without remedy.[74]

Among the familiar negatives spawned by social media and chiefly affecting younger users are bullying, harassment, sharing of harmful suggestions and information about self-harming and suicide, spreading of false information, libelling and shaming individuals, conspiracy theories, opportunities for sexual grooming of minors, malignant forms of pornography, and publication of material that is egregiously offensive and disturbing. Much of this could be prevented by abolishing anonymity on social media, requiring that access to it be predicated on authenticated personal information. The counterargument usually given is that there are people and circumstances where anonymity is important – release of information which is in the public interest but which would bring severe repercussions on the whistle-blower, people in danger if their identity were known, and the like. On balance, it is arguable that the vile nature of so much on social media makes loss of anonymity a worthwhile cost to pay.

One major example of potential social media harm is its effect on democracy.[75] It is a standard feature of democratic politics that those seeking voters' support should not only put a programme before them but try to persuade them of its merits.

It is equally standard and legitimate for them to criticize their opponents' proposals, and for others – newspapers, interest groups, individuals – to comment on, criticize, oppose, or endorse what the politicians are saying. This once happened on hustings in the form of platforms in the public square and soap-boxes, but hustings evolved to include television studios and advertisements, still publicly available to all and sundry. Social media and their microtargeting capability change that; there are now hustings for selected groups only, sending them messages which, if they contain falsehoods or misleading statements, cannot be called out and challenged by others because these others cannot see them.

The above picture of a vigorous democratic debate on open hustings, summoning the enfranchised to make a choice, is of course idealized. In practice politics has always involved spin and dirty tricks, half-truths and untruths, distortion, propaganda, *ad hominem* attacks on individuals rather than their ideas, all aimed at inflating the positives of one party and undermining the other parties' credibility. Propaganda is a tool of politics and has always been so, by its nature not pretending to be a medium of truth and accuracy. There have always been demagogues playing on the hopes, fears, prejudices, and desires, and on the anger or the nationalistic or patriotic sentiment, of populaces; Benito Mussolini and Adolf Hitler stand out as recent historical paradigms. Less obvious candidates for demagoguery are the owners of newspapers which push their owner's agenda, often in undisguisedly propagandistic ways. The British tabloid press is an especially egregious example of this.

All the traditional phenomena of spin, propaganda, and manipulation put pressure on the reliability of the democratic process. But since the beginning of the twenty-first century these techniques have been taken to an entirely new level of effectiveness by social media. Big Data analytics potentiates not just demagoguery but forms of hidden persuasion, also enabled by computer hacking. There were claims of actual or attempted interference by Russian agencies in the US presidential elections of 2016 and 2020, and similarly in the Brexit referendum in the UK in 2016 and various European elections in 2017 and 2019. Fake news was a salient feature of political events in this period, linked to the interference in question. It is easy to get carried away by conspiracy theories, including those that go on to indict the so-called 'deep state' in various countries for influencing and sometimes interfering with the governments there; but in these cases there are genuine grounds for concern.

This is illustrated by a report in the *New York Times* for 15 March 2017 that stated:

> In a development that can only heighten the distrust between American and Russian authorities on cybersecurity, the Justice Department on Wednesday charged two Russian intelligence officers with directing a sweeping criminal conspiracy that broke into 500 million Yahoo accounts in 2014 ... Details of the wide-ranging attack come as the United States government is investigating other Russian cyberattacks against American targets, including the theft of emails last year from the Democratic National Committee and attempts to break in to state election systems. Investigators are also examining communications between associates of President Trump and Russian officials that occurred during the presidential campaign ... On Wednesday, prosecutors unsealed an indictment containing 47 criminal charges against the two agents of Russia's Federal Security Service, or F.S.B., as well as two outside hackers ...[76]

On the same day, the BBC announced a collaboration with a journalism project called 'CrossCheck', set up by First Draft News, 'to verify and debunk fake stories surrounding the upcoming French elections'. The first false story they exposed was that presidential candidate Emmanuel Macron was receiving campaign finance from Saudi Arabia. Concerns in France about fundamentalist Islamic terrorism, given the horrifying Charlie Hebdo and Bataclan attacks, would make any such link inflammatory, given Saudi support for the Wahhabi form of Islam often associated with extremism.[77]

Reports such as these doubtless do no more than touch the tips of icebergs. The better-known case of Big Data analytics is not only troubling in itself as applied to elections and opinion formation – in medical research and elsewhere in science it is a boon – but it demonstrates the technical power that lies behind these other cases also.

Consider the example of the data company known as Cambridge Analytica, since closed down because of the negative publicity it garnered from its role in the Trump and Brexit campaigns of 2016. By harvesting huge amounts of social media data and analysing it using machine-learning AI, Cambridge Analytica created fine-grained psychometric profiles of individual voters enabling it to identify their emotional triggers, and on that basis sent them tailored messages and advertisements. The Trump campaign paid Cambridge Analytica in excess of $6 million to influence swing voters by these means – a cheaper yet far more effective means of reaching them than scattergun public advertising. A report in the UK's *Observer* newspaper on 26 February 2017 revealed that Cambridge Analytica was instrumental in the success of the pro-Brexit campaign in the UK too; one of those who had funded the pro-Brexit campaign claimed that Cambridge Analytica's 'world class AI had helped them gain unprecedented levels of engagement' among voters, adding, 'AI won it for Leave' ('Leave' being the generic pro-Brexit designation).[78]

The international dimension of interference and manipulation predicated on Big Data – keep in mind that Big Data is the fruit harvested from us by social media platforms and sold to end-users such as Cambridge Analytica – is well illustrated by the connection between the Trump and Brexit cases. The Communications Director of Leave told the *Observer* that Robert Mercer, billionaire owner of *Breitbart News*, part-owner of Cambridge Analytica, and a friend of one of the principals in the Leave endeavour, had offered the services of the company to the Leave campaign at no cost because of the 'shared goals' of Breitbart, Trump, and Brexit: he stated that 'What they were trying to do in the US and what we were trying to do had massive parallels. We shared a lot of information.'

In describing the process the *Observer* captured the unease not only of critics but of those who had themselves employed it:

The strategy involved harvesting data from people's Facebook and other social media profiles and then using machine learning to 'spread' through their networks. [The Communications Director of Leave] admitted the technology and level of information it gathered from people was 'creepy.' He said the campaign used this information, combined with artificial intelligence, to decide who to target with highly individualized advertisements . . . A leading expert on the impact of technology on elections called the revelation 'extremely disturbing and quite sinister . . . it undermines the whole bases of our electoral system, that we should have a level playing field . . . We have no idea what people are being shown or not, which makes it frankly sinister'.[79]

A number of points of concern are illustrated by this case. One is about transparency, not only in the sense that individuals have a right to know that they are being profiled and what their profile looks like, but what aspects of it prompt the information, advertising, and messaging they therefore receive. In the case of political messaging such targeting is even less acceptable; it might, for example, be identifying and exploiting racial prejudices, or inflaming religious or nationalist sentiment. Political messaging by its nature is partisan and tendentious, but if it is being fine-tuned to pull an individual's 'emotional triggers' it amounts to manipulation, and manipulation of which its victims are unaware. This is further subversion of what should be an open process. If you found that you had been targeted with messages, it would be of great relevance to know who they are from and what they are seeking to achieve by eliciting your support, so that you can evaluate them properly and consider your response. If the content of the message is being inserted by means of your emotional reactions, and in such a way that you do not fully appreciate either that fact itself or its implications, you are being manipulated.

The easiest targets for hidden persuaders are ingenuous persuadees. It was not an original discovery by Daniel Kahneman that people divide into what he calls 'fast' (he means 'hasty', 'shallow') and 'slow' (he means 'careful', 'judicious') thinkers.[80] Bertrand Russell famously said, 'Most people would rather die than think, and most people do,' and an anecdote about the 1952 presidential candidate Adlai Stevenson sums the matter up well; told by an enthusiastic supporter that he was sure to receive the votes of 'every thinking person in the United States' Stevenson replied, 'I'm glad to hear it; but I need a majority.' Campaign managers have long known that the more manipulable of the populace are in the majority, and have acted accordingly. Joseph Goebbels summarized the basic method: repeat something often enough and loud enough and most people will soon believe it. By means of social media, the use of Big Data and hacking potentiates the range, speed, and power of this old and well-tried process millions of times over. False claims and unfulfillable promises have their desired effect on first being issued, and their effect is not nullified by subsequent modification or withdrawal; one might say that falsehood-bombing the populace has become the alternative to truth and debate about truth. Social media has made this as easy as it is now widespread.

Among critics of democracy are those who fear that democracy is merely the anteroom to anarchy, on the grounds that it can too readily collapse into 'ochlocracy' or mob-rule. Plato was one such; he regarded it as inevitable that the uninformed, prejudiced, self-interested, emotionally-driven many would take power and that bad government would therefore follow. History has some extreme examples of this to show, in the form of revolutionary mobs creating a chaos into which tyranny soon steps to take control. *Representative* democracy is one of the forms of democracy devised to respect the ultimate political authority of the people while ensuring also that adequate government can be achieved.[81] In our present day highly sophisticated social media techniques are employed, by partisan interests, to target precisely the prejudiced, self-interested, emotionally-driven – and not infrequently uninformed – attitudes of different groups, to aggregate them into voting for an outcome which is the partisan interest's own preference. In the distortions that democracy has suffered, new manipulators have found a way to pervert its aims by means of social media.

Whatever other remedies and safeguards can be devised to protect the democratic process from the harms that social media can be used to create, the following two at least are crucial. First, no political advertising and messaging should be microtargeted; it should all be public and scrutable, so that anything false or misleading can be challenged. And second, all messaging should be clearly labelled to show from whom, or on whose behalf, the message is sent. This tells all voters who is saying what, and on that basis they have a chance of making better choices at the ballot box.

The recent history of technological innovation has been a very crowded one. With steam power, the harnessing of electricity, the internal combustion engine, the telegraph, telephone, heavier-than-air flight, splitting the atom, computing, the internet and World Wide Web, and hard on the latter's heels the high-speed mushrooming of chip-based power both miniature in size and huge in capacity, the world has seen more rapid and more revolutionary change than in almost any previous period of history. The developments have branched off one another and mutually potentiated each other like a rapidly spreading network of tentacles. The sheer scale and speed of development in all these spheres has made it hard to catch one's breath and evaluate their implications. Just one of the fast-ramifying multiple aspects of any one of AI, genetics, and social media would pose a large enough problem on its own; we have all of them to deal with simultaneously. It would be more rather than less correct to say that humankind is not in control of what it is doing; it is on a bicycle without brakes hurtling down a mountainside. Arguably, the very difficult problem of climate change is easier to deal with than the spreading, escaping potentials of current technological developments. This would be so even without the malignant pressure of the self-interest Law. Take that into account too, and the question has to be this: once one has taken into account the

113

counterbalancing effect of the good potentials in these developments, and the chance that countermeasures to some of the bad
potentials might be engineered also, what does the global
community need to do to get a grip on what is happening, in
hopes of avoiding at least the worst of the possible negative
outcomes that can be foreseen?

3

JUSTICE AND RIGHTS

In the Introduction it was observed that the deficits of economic, social, and legal justice in the world, and the widespread denial or outright violation of rights in many places, look like a miscellany, but they are connected, and play an important part in exacerbating the difficulty of achieving global consensus on how to respond to global threats.

The briefest of surveys illustrates how various and intractable the problems are. Almost nowhere has gender equality been achieved; girls and women are subordinated or at very least hampered by social, cultural, and religious traditions and attitudes everywhere, developed countries not excluded. In many places there is denial of the most basic rights to personal and private life; homosexuality is outlawed in seventy countries – exposed to the death penalty in some – and homosexuals suffer social opprobrium and harassment in yet more. Problems current and historical over differences in religion range from discrimination to fatal violence. Historical legacies of religious differences are of a piece with the continuing effects of historical wrongs such as genocides and slavery. In most countries of the world there are at least questions, and in most of them problems, about access to remedies at law, protection of rights, and exercise of liberties. Economic justice is a vexed issue that ranges from individual economic oppression in circumstances of income inequality to extreme poverty suffered by large populations, to the weighting of the international economic and trade order in favour of wealthier nations. Sometimes the scarcely visible versions of these problems do as much damage, if in different ways, as gross and obvious versions. The fact that hundreds of millions of people, as individuals and as collectives, fail to benefit from access to justice and the observance of rights, contributes directly and otherwise to the problem addressed in these pages: the world's inability to unite in the face of difficulties that cut across physical borders and invisible boundaries.

I look first at examples of these problems, and then at what is meant by concepts of justice and rights, to clarify the grounds there are for asserting that these latter are deficient or absent in a given setting if they are indeed so. This is necessary because there are circumstances of (for example) inequality that are not an artefact of injustice, and circumstances where cultural traditions ignore what other traditions regard as entitlements but without thereby violating any human rights. The claim that some state of affairs is unjust, or that the rights of some person or people are being denied, requires solid footing in what the concepts mean. They are large concepts, over whose definition and boundaries much theoretical debate rages; but the practical question of how things are in the world and what might be done about it requires that there be sufficient consensus on their meaning.

Consider first the question of poverty. According to the 'Our World in Data' project of the educational charity Global Change Data Lab, 85 per cent of the world's population in the year 2019 lived on less than $30 a day, 66 per cent lived on less than $10 a day, and 10 per cent on less than $2 a day, this last being the level of *extreme* poverty.[1] Although poverty has been declining dramatically in the course of the last thirty years – in 1990 more than two billion people lived in extreme poverty, a number now predicted to fall below 500 million by 2030 – it remains that one in every ten people on the planet is living a hand-to-mouth existence.

Those are the raw figures. But as one would expect, the situation is more complex. What of those living on $3 a day, or $5? Their lot is not so far different from those under the $2 level, and the nature of the poverty is relevant, because it can be experienced in different versions of what the United Nations poverty index describes as 'multidimensional poverty'.[2] In addition to the crude figure of available income, the UN measures health, education, and standard of living to define as 'deprived' anyone who experiences problems in a third of the following areas combined: if anyone under the age of seventy is undernourished, or if a family has lost a child under the age of eighteen in the five years before the survey, they fall into the health dimension of poverty. If no member of a household over the age of twelve has completed six years of school, or if any school-aged child is not attending school, they fall into the education dimension of poverty. If a household cooks with dung, wood, or charcoal, lacks electricity, lives in a structure built from inadequate materials (by Sustainable Development Goal – SDG – standards), lacks SDG minimum standard sanitation, is more than a thirty-minute round-trip walk to a clean water supply, and does not own at least one of a radio, television, telephone, computer, animal cart, bicycle, motorbike, refrigerator, car, or truck, they fall into the category of the 'multidimensionally poor'.[3]

The aim of combating poverty and – in ways that are environmentally sustainable – improving the quality of life for the world's peoples, an aim originally enshrined in the UN's

'Millennium Goals' project adopted in 2000, was reinforced by the Sustainable Development Goals set out by the UN's General Assembly in 2016. The seventeen goals include the ending of poverty and hunger; the promotion of health and education; the provision of clean water, energy, and decent employment; and justice and gender equality.[4] All of them, and not least this last, turn on questions of justice.

The immediate reaction of some to mention of the absence of 'television, telephone, computer' and the rest in talk of 'multidimensional poverty' will be that the UN is setting the bar high for an acceptable standard of living. They might point out that there are hunter-gatherer societies still in existence, for example, in the Amazon forest, who not only lack such amenities but whose acquisition of them would be regarded as a tragedy, since it would entail the destruction of their way of life. This reaction would doubtless be modified, though, when it is pointed out that by the UN's reckoning 1.3 billion people are multidimensionally poor, and more than 80 per cent of these are deprived in five of the ways described simultaneously. Out of a world population of seven billion, 5.9 billion are deprived in at least one of these categories. These are astonishingly high figures.

The great majority of the world's poor live in sub-Saharan Africa and south Asia. Most of them live in rural areas. Females suffer more from the effects of deprivation than males. Among the deprivations suffered by the 1.3 billion multidimensionally poor are factors that should make even the most hardened of self-interested people sit up and take notice: many of these poor cannot get access to vaccination against communicable diseases, and constitute both a reservoir of these diseases and a breeding-ground for mutations in the pathogens that cause them. In the Covid-19 pandemic starting in 2020 there were major anxieties about vaccine-resistant mutations occurring in populations where immunization against permutated strains was slow or patchy. The presence of more than a billion multidimensionally poor in the world constitutes a permanent version of this situation. Accordingly, even the most callously indifferent to the struggles of the poor might think of the danger that world poverty presents to themselves.

The poorer one is, the harder it is to escape poverty. A child brought up in a slum, a shanty town, a favela, amidst overcrowding, unsanitary conditions, high infant mortality, and crime, might have better prospects in life by becoming a criminal than by hoping for a 'normal' career. In some senses it might be more bearable to be poor in a country where the hardships of poverty – insecurity, hunger, disease, and other features of the condition – are shared by many others. Being poor in a developed country carries other burdens. When everyone is wearing rags, shabby clothes do not matter. Publicly carrying the negative marks of one's position in the scheme of things adds psychological exhaustion to the mixture.

In developed countries poverty is a relative notion; in the UK, taking it as an example of a developed country, the poverty line is 60 per cent of median household income. In the year 2020 that meant any household with an income below £17,760 per annum was in poverty. That is $67 a day. About 23 per cent of the population – close to 12 million people, including 4.5 million children, live in poverty by this measure. The number in 'deep poverty', living on incomes below half the poverty line, is about 4.5 million, a number that grew as a result of the Covid-19 pandemic. One difference between poverty in a developed economy and in regions of endemic poverty such as sub-Saharan Africa is that poor people in the former are likely to be rich in liabilities – debts, unpaid rent, and bills – and excluded from access to many opportunities and social goods such as education and community participation which the majority enjoy and which, in a developed country, are necessary for escaping poverty.

Once again, those indifferent to the plight of the poor are invited to consult their own self-interest: inequality and poverty in developed countries are toxic and destabilizing. Resentment and perceptions of injustice are flammable sentiments. Those who value their own material advantages do well to ensure that others have them too.

But appeals to self-interest should not be the only resource of anti-poverty campaigners. There is an intrinsic moral imperative here, to the effect that where the means exist to alleviate hardship and suffering, hardship and suffering should be alleviated. It is a culpable matter that in the same society some should be living in conspicuous luxury while others sleep on the streets in winter and rely on hand-outs of food. This applies even if the reason for the disparity is not that the economic order is weighted in favour of those who start with advantages in wealth, position, and access. Even if there were no such structural injustices, the disparity would be unacceptable. Battered by the elements, King Lear had an epiphany:

> Poor naked wretches, whereso'er you are,
> That bide the pelting of this pitiless storm,
> How shall your houseless heads and unfed sides,
> Your looped and windowed raggedness, defend you
> From seasons such as these? Oh, I have ta'en
> Too little care of this! Take physic, pomp.
> Expose thyself to feel what wretches feel,
> That thou mayst shake the superflux to them
> And show the heavens more just.[5]

Of course, both in Shakespeare's time and in developed countries today the wealth disparities are not adventitious, not purely a matter of greater talent, harder work, and more useful products bringing their rewards to some while others, including the feckless and incapable, languish. A privately educated scion of a wealthy family might end by sleeping rough as a heroin addict, and that has happened; but the odds are far otherwise. It is practically a cliché to assert that advantages of family, education, and connections play a significant role in creating and maintaining inequalities in society. Nevertheless, by itself this might not constitute an injustice, and would not do so if the possession of advantages by some did not rely directly or indirectly on the immiseration of others. The question is whether the way a society is organized *unjustly* results in poverty for some.

One way to think about this is to look at an example where factors contributing to poverty can be identified and their sources distinguished. Consider Bangladesh, one of the poorest countries in the world. Answers to the question why it is poor almost always include: vulnerability to floods and droughts, overpopulation, lack of infrastructure, low literacy levels, historical exploitation, weak institutions, political instability, religion-promoted social backwardness, a minimal export sector, and little tradition of entrepreneurship. Some of these factors remain, though at time of writing Bangladesh is a country making striking progress, overtaking Pakistan, of which it was once part and against which it fought a war of independence, in growth and per capita income – partly because restraints on population growth are working. Among the factors that have turned the country round since 2006 is the success of the micro-loans initiative of the Grameen Bank, the brainchild of Muhammad Yunus for which he was awarded the Nobel Peace Prize.[6] Increased educational opportunities for girls and a greater voice for women in both private and public has resulted among other things in more children being educated, infant mortality decreasing, and overall life expectancy increasing.

For present purposes the point to note is the contrast between two very different kinds of factor on which Bangladesh's poverty has been blamed. One includes droughts, floods, overpopulation, religion; the other includes lack of infrastructure, low literacy levels, weak institutions, and little tradition of entrepreneurship. The latter can be summed up as a consequence of historical exploitation – the fact that the former colonial rulers of the region that is now Bangladesh did not bequeath the infrastructure, education system, and practices of government and commerce that would have given Bangladesh a better start as an independent country when it became one. On the contrary, the colonial rulers – the British Raj in India – were there to extract advantage, not confer it. By any standard the judgment that at least part of Bangladesh's problem is the result of exploitation – exploitation being the act of profiting by imposing a cost or loss on another or others – is inescapable.

The point generalizes. Sustained historical disadvantages affect many formerly colonized countries as they affect the descendants of slaves and oppressed minorities. The presence of other factors – in Bangladesh's case the climate and population size relative to the country's small land area – exacerbates matters, making it harder to combat the structural barriers erected by two centuries of exploitation.

In developed economies the reasons for inequality, and ultimately of poverty for some, are likewise attributable to two different kinds of factor. Talent, hard work, and luck play their part; no question of injustice arises there. Inherited advantages of wealth and property, and the effect they have of skewing the distribution of wealth by attracting more wealth to those who already have it than to those who have less of it – a biblical situation – is not intrinsically unjust if it does not also erect barriers to the talent and hard work that might give an opportunity to flourish to those without initial advantages. But alas the fact that people have very different starting points does indeed mean that the rest of the playing field is uneven also. Political influence, monopoly positions, helpful personal connections, possession of resources, and access to information that give a built-in advantage of the 'first mover' kind, add to the host of other benefits large and small – such as access to the quality of education, mobility, health care, even nutrition – that make a difference also. The result is that society is structurally skewed in favour of those who already have advantages. If no redistribution occurs through graduated taxation and some control on inheritance of assets, the accumulation of more and more wealth in fewer and fewer hands is inevitable. The overall tendency for this to happen under capitalism is accepted, and the resulting inequality is applauded by some on the grounds that it offers incentives to people to work and innovate to increase their own wealth. But this means that inequality, and its concomitant effect of poverty for a significant fraction of the populace, are built into the system itself.

Matters are in fact worse than the foregoing sketch suggests, for it does not mention gender, ethnicity, disability, and age as other sources of disadvantage, not only in themselves for obvious reasons, but because society does not do enough to ensure against their acting as competitive disadvantages. Now add that economic cycles, automation in industry, political changes affecting taxation and spending policies, and other factors, can increase the chronic built-in level of underlying unemployment in the economy, resulting in poverty for the medium- and long-term unemployed and their families. In the first decades of the twenty-first century a major enforced move of labour into the 'gig' economy of temporary and part-time piecework, insecure and without standard employment benefits, added to levels of functional poverty, institutionalizing yet another factor in the system's weighting against the less advantaged.

Wealthy people influence their societies and the politics of their societies; the poorer people get, the less of a voice they have, until forced onto the streets to demonstrate, riot, or revolt as their only way of being heard. On trends apparent in the first decade of the twenty-first century, it was predicted that by 2030 two-thirds of global wealth would be owned by 1 per cent of the world's population.[7] While at the same time overall global poverty is decreasing, as mentioned above, the 1.3 billion people in extreme poverty at time of writing face additional problems from the effects of climate change – to cite Bangladesh again: it is at risk of losing 11 per cent of its land area to rising sea levels, displacing 15–20 million people; and already salinization of the soil and water in coastal areas is impacting crop production and fresh water availability.[8] So for those many for whom the statistics of poverty are an abstraction, matters are only set to get worse.

There is much more to say about the sources and effects of poverty, both as to pragmatic considerations relating to its effects as a drag on the world economy and a danger to the world's population, and as to the moral fact – which by itself should be enough – that there is an abundance of resources in the world, leaving no excuse for a situation in which anyone suffers the hardships of hunger and deprivation.[9] Strategies for expediting the reduction in world poverty, and in particular for addressing it in the regions where it is most prevalent – sub-Saharan Africa and south Asia – involve not just aid, investment, and resolution of conflicts, but strategies of governance which reach right into the details of life so that the poor can help themselves: for one example, inexpensive public transport for people to access education, jobs, and markets; for another example, land registration which allows people to own the land they live on, giving them the confidence and security to build a dwelling out of brick instead of shanty materials, and to plant some vegetables and maize.[10] On the principle of 'better teach a person to fish than give him a fish to eat' it is the details, sometimes unexpected and seen only in the corner of the eye, that make a helping hand work.

If taking action against poverty were left to the charitable instincts of individuals only, or to individual governments only, progress would be slow if it happened at all. The international bodies working on poverty reduction are the principal actors coordinating the effort. A number of non-governmental agencies do sterling work in this endeavour; the premier effort is the United Nations' Sustainable Development Goals project, among which ending poverty and hunger, and doing it in conjunction with action on climate, the environment, and issues of justice and rights, are at the top of the list.[11] The seventeenth of the seventeen goals – 'Partnership' – makes the right statement of the obvious: 'If all countries are to achieve the goals, international cooperation is vital'. One of the many reasons for this is that the goals are interdependent; ending poverty requires growth, growth has to be sustainable to meet climate change targets, education and improvement in quality of life require peace, as does working for better population health and the provision of infrastructure and amenities such as clean water; and these are all, once again, conditions of ending the various dimensions of multidimensional poverty. There are no loose ends in the net of dependencies among the goals.

But that means that progress towards the overall realization of the goals is vulnerable to the kinds of interruption to which each goal is independently vulnerable. One hint of this is given by the reduction in the UK government overseas aid budget in 2021 because of economic strains caused by Brexit and the Covid-19 pandemic. Another is that, in the same year, negotiations between the US and the Taliban in Afghanistan, in preparation for US withdrawal from the region, prompted reminders that in previous periods of Taliban control traditional restrictions were enforced on women and girls, including denial of education for the latter, and in general the civil liberties climate of the country became very bleak, a standard concomitant of fundamentalist religious regimes.

One country reducing aid, another imposing hardline religious orthopraxy, are grit in the machine; it does not take much for a major and complex project to suffer disruption. Pandemic disease, a major war, a global economic crisis precipitated by an event like the 2008 financial markets meltdown, are perennial risks. International cooperation has to be such that it anticipates the inevitability of obstacles like these, but is determined to achieve the goals nevertheless.

Goal five of the Sustainable Development Goals is 'gender equality'. The intention of the phrase is clear, though preferable would be 'gender equity' because whereas there are many important respects in which it goes without saying that equality should be sought – pay, access to education, participation in political activities, and more – there are respects in which differential provision is needed. There are some health provision requirements, such as maternity services, and the number and kind of restroom facilities available in places of public resort, where gender equality, strictly understood, would be unfair. Of

much larger moment is the fact that both developed and traditional societies are, each in their own way, structurally biased
against women.

In developed economies the shape of the working week
poses an immediate barrier to women with children, unless
they have available, can afford, and are willing to make use of,
childcare facilities comprehensive enough to put them on the
same footing as men in the workplace. The usual result for
women who have children and who wish to or need to work is
to do so part-time, in jobs that are in general less well paid and
with fewer prospects than full-time jobs. In employment and
career terms, the price paid by many women for motherhood
is to fall behind in career terms, or to fall out completely.
Resuming a career after a number of years, when children are
at school or have left home, is usually difficult.[12] On a wide
range of measures, from career prospects to income – even to
hours of sleep – motherhood brings substantial reductions. In
comparison to the value attached to having and raising children these are less important, but not irrelevant, considerations for most women.

In traditional societies views about the role of women, principally that their chief functions are maternal and domestic, and
that the management of their lives belongs to their fathers,
brothers, and husbands, are familiar. In every society and historical period there are and have been many women of powerful
personality who in practice rule the men in their circle, and
often by extension the community in which they live, whatever
the norms are officially supposed to be. But this does not one
whit compensate for the systemic weighting of social and
economic structures in favour of men.

In traditional societies, and to a lesser but still major extent in
developed societies, the exclusion of women from a full and

unrestricted opportunity to participate economically, educationally, culturally, and politically represents an enormous loss of talent, a huge waste of creativity and energy, for humankind.

What is extraordinary is that moves to remedy this situation began so recently in history, and even where they have been most successful they are still incomplete. Perhaps because of the smaller size and lesser muscular strength of females, and the confining character of pregnancy, nursing, and infant care, coupled with the correlative opposites in males, early hominin communities reflected the trend of male dominance of social groups seen in many species of animals. By the time this emerged into consciously organized social structures, the view that women are 'inferior' had come to seem a truth as obvious as that the sun rises in the east. That would explain why the author of a gynaecological text in the ancient Hippocratic corpus felt it necessary to admonish fellow physicians, 'We must not disbelieve women with regard to childbirth. For they constantly and repeatedly make assertions about everything, and nothing can persuade them, neither argument nor evidence, that they are ignorant of what is happening in their bodies.'[13] The text shows that his colleagues were inclined to dismiss women's views on the very female enterprise of pregnancy and birth because they – the male physicians – knew better; the ultimate in 'mansplaining'.

That was still the case at the end of the nineteenth century, as John Studd's accounts of sometimes brutal and sadistic gynaecological practice in that period shows.[14] Among other abusive 'treatments' clitoral and labial cauterization and clitoridectomy were employed to deal with cases of 'masturbation, menstrual madness, neurasthenia, nymphomania, and "all cases of insanity"', these latter including – in cases cited by one of the worst offenders – one woman's desire to leave her husband, and another young woman's propensity to quarrel with her mother.[15]

Some attitudes to women turned on fear of their sexuality and the belief that they are dangerous temptresses – as Tertullian famously put it, they were 'the gateway to the devil'. Religious practices (not confined to Islam) of requiring women to be covered up, or to be sequestered from public view, are as often cited to be a protection for men from the temptation women represent as protecting women from being preyed upon by men. Either way, the remark that women in ancient Athens were at last able to go out into the streets unattended when they had reached the stage – which means, the age – of being asked 'whose mother are you?' rather than 'whose wife are you?' were not thus free because of enhanced status but because of diminished value; their chief worth lay in their reproductive role, and when their fecundity – or sexual attractiveness: whichever came first – diminished, their standing followed suit.[16]

It is easy to see that living a circumscribed and undervalued life without escape would be stressful and unpleasant at least, productive of physical and mental ill-health, and intolerable if coupled with abuse. A combination of belief about female inferiority – to which the great majority of women themselves subscribed, so indoctrinated were they by social attitudes – and male incomprehension of female physical and emotional complexity, resulted in a framework of social, moral, and medical practices relating to them, premised in essence on the idea that 'a woman is a failed man' (as Aristotle put it – and Freud's view 2,500 years later was not much different), which are in themselves abusive. A survey of the history of thinking about female mental illness and in particular 'hysteria' gives a sobering view of this.[17] Hysteria is described as early as 1900 BCE in the Kahun Papyri as spontaneous migration of the uterus around the body; ancient Egyptian treatment of the disorder involved applying acrid fumes to the nose to drive, and fragrant fumes to the vulva to entice, the uterus to move back downwards if it had risen, or vice versa if it had fallen – a practice maintained through Greek medicine and indeed all the way to the nineteenth-century CE practice of ladies carrying smelling salts in their handbags, the underlying idea (no longer *literally* believed) being to reposition a uterus which had risen into the upper abdomen or chest causing stifling, fainting feelings of anxiety and panic.[18]

Victimization as witches put older women unprotected by any association with men – thus, widows and spinsters – in danger of scapegoating by communities, even by individuals, when misfortunes fell or some situation of social anxiety arose. Although mortality rates for boys and men from all causes are higher than for girls and women, and they die earlier in the natural course of life also, peril for girls and women is greater in domestic circumstances.[19] In the United States three out of every four domestic homicide victims are women, and a recent World Health Organization report states that a third of women worldwide have experienced domestic violence at some point in their lives – a shocking statistic.[20] In England and Wales two women are murdered every week by intimate partners, while the UN estimates that globally 137 women are killed in domestic incidents every day – nearly six an hour.[21]

The further matter of *sexual* violence, rape, harassment, abuse, enforced prostitution, and enslavement has to be added to an already devastating picture. Across the range from discrimination in employment to the worst excesses of violent and sexual crimes, with all the concomitants such as women's fears about walking alone in a street at night or whether to trust a new acquaintance met at a social gathering, the situation for women in our world is unconscionable. Yet even to get to the current far-from-ideal point in developed societies, the struggle has been enormous.

The effort to achieve what was appropriately called *female emancipation* in modern times owes part of its immediate inspiration to the anti-slavery campaigns that began in the eighteenth century, and for workers' rights in the nineteenth century. Women participated in them, learned from them, contributed to them, and did so under the double handicap that being women imposed; for they had all the disabilities of the men alongside whom they worked in these causes, together with all the disabilities of being women too, in a manner reminiscent of Ginger Rogers's remark that she did everything Fred Astaire did, but 'backwards and in high heels'.[22]

An important reason for recalling the history of women's rights campaigns is the light they shed on what would potentiate social and economic advances in the contemporary developing world.[23] Even the most elementary education for girls, sufficient for basic literacy and numeracy, is known to reduce both the size of families and infant mortality in Africa, to enhance the prospects of children attaining education levels greater than that of their mothers, and to decrease rates of HIV infection. One factor in this is that where women are allowed to own – as opposed to being – property, HIV infection rates decrease because women are not merely handed from father to husband, or from the graveside of one husband to the bed of another, but if orphaned or widowed can choose to manage on their own behalf for themselves and their children. As a way of shortening the road to female emancipation in the developing world even as the unfinished campaign for it in the developed world continues, it is useful to have an overview of how long it took, and what it took, to get as far as women in the developed world have come.

In North America and Europe in the eighteenth and nine-teenth centuries it was an obvious step from the campaign to end slavery to a campaign for women's rights. Writing about the effects on women of involvement in the anti-slavery movement, Elizabeth Cady Stanton wrote:

> In the early Anti-Slavery conventions, the broad principles of human rights were so exhaustively discussed, justice, liberty, and equality, so clearly taught, that the women who crowded to listen readily learned the lesson of freedom for themselves, and early began to take part in the debates and business affairs of all asso-ciations. Woman not only felt every pulsation of man's heart for freedom, and by her enthusiasm inspired the glowing eloquence that maintained him through the struggle, but earnestly advo-cated with her own lips human freedom and equality.[24]

A second feature of women's involvement in anti-slavery campaigning was that it gave the lie to traditional views about women's supposed intellectual and physical incapacities. The denigratory view – an apt term in the context – of women was that they were incapable of understanding complex problems or thinking logically about them; incapable of long hours of mental work; too like children in being emotional, trivial, distractible, and ill-informed; too physically and psychologically fragile to be given the responsibilities typically shouldered by men – all this quite seriously believed, and scarcely ever challenged by striking examples to the contrary, of women labouring in the fields, in factories, the physical and mental demands of mother-hood that a man would scarcely bear for a day, and much besides.

The story of the women's rights effort goes back to isolated but remarkable voices in the seventeenth century and before – Aphra Behn is cited as an early example – but the first major voice belongs to Mary Wollstonecraft, whose *Vindication of the Rights of Woman* marked an epoch in feminism.[25] In the dedicatory epistle to that work she wrote, 'Contending for the rights of women, my main argument is built on this simple principle, that if she be not prepared by education to become the companion of man, she will stop the progress of knowledge, for truth must be common to all, or it will be inefficacious with respect to its influence on general practice.'[26]

It took women in the UK until 1928 to get voting rights on an equal basis with men. It happened a decade earlier in the US; the Nineteenth Amendment, passed in 1919, laconically states, 'The right of citizens of the United States to vote shall not be denied or abridged by the United States or by any State on account of sex.' This was only the beginning for the next major step: in the case of the US, the (yet unfinished) battle for an Equal Rights Amendment, and from the 1960s onwards a determined effort to change attitudes as well as practices affecting women in society and the workplace perforce continued – because getting the vote had not by itself shifted the deeply ingrained and institutionalized patriarchal attitudes of society and its attendant structures.

The indivisibility of liberty efforts is exemplified by the fact that 'second wave' feminist activism in 1960s and '70s America was in significant part inspired by the Civil Rights movement, and had the same underlying rationale: that although slavery no longer existed, 100 years after its abolition racism and apartheid still did. The question of *getting* rights, and the question of getting rights *applied*, are two different matters; and the examples of slaves and women in the US suggest a pattern – that once a framework, usually of statute, is in place, the task of changing attitudes and practices has then to begin, because they are every bit as imprisoning as the absence of enabling laws, or the presence of disabling laws. This is significant for thinking about how genuine emancipation might be achieved for women in the developing world.

The eventual achievements of first wave feminism – from Wollstonecraft to Millicent Fawcett and the Pankhursts – is a matter of history. But property rights, education, and the vote dismantled very little of the patriarchal structure of society and economy, and women's lives continued to be no more fulfilling – indeed, because of education and the aspirations it encouraged, far less so – than they had always been. Simone de Beauvoir's *The Second Sex* (1949) and Betty Friedan's *The Feminine Mystique* (1963) triggered a second wave of feminist activism, aimed at gaining equality of legal, social, and economic rights, and at confronting the sexual objectification of women (demonstrations at the 1969 Miss America contest were an eloquent statement of intent on that score).[27] In the economic boom after 1945, with a baby boom alongside and the growth of suburban living, associated with the advertiser-led myth of the happy housewife with her labour-saving vacuum cleaner, washing machine, and refrigerator, causes for dissatisfaction were as deep as understanding of them was – to begin with – shallow, not least by women themselves, who as Friedan showed were perplexed and alienated from themselves by the belief that they *should* be feeling content. When women began talking to each other about their situation, increasingly aided by books that examined and articulated their discontents – books by Ann Oakley, Germaine Greer, Kate Millett, and others – a confident and vocal campaign resulted.

There were other factors in the mixture: the contraceptive pill was approved by the Food and Drug Administration in 1960 (initially only for married women), the anti-Vietnam War campaigns and the Civil Rights movement were shifting the landscape in major ways; the gay rights endeavour was galvanized by a police raid on the Stonewall Inn in New York's Greenwich Village on 28 June 1969, provoking a riot; oppression and marginalization were no longer tolerable.[28] So-called 'women's lib' was a major part of these upheavals.

The movement had many successes. It produced significant shifts in the professions and employment generally, in politics, education, and popular culture, and gave a major boost to women's self-perception and sense of possibilities. The list of achievements, from the Equal Pay Act of 1963 through affirmative action rights, no-fault divorce, outlawing of marital rape, family planning services, and *Roe v Wade* 1972 on abortion, is long.

Some commentators suggest that the ebbing of feminist activism in the 1980s was in part a natural pause after the efforts and achievements of the 1960 and '70s, and in part a result of disagreements among liberal and radical feminists about, for chief examples, sexuality, pornography, and sex work/prostitution – using the virgule for these two terms exemplifies the difference of opinion at issue; for radical feminists 'prostitution' is the product of male-dominated society's objectification and exploitation of women, while other feminists believe in solidarity with the rights of women (and men) who are 'sex workers'.

The beginning of 'third wave feminism' is assigned to the early 1990s and associated by some with Naomi Wolf's *The Beauty Myth*, the film *Thelma and Louise*, and the punk culture 'Riot grrrl' phenomenon that began in the US's Pacific Northwest.[29] The movement itself is much more disparate than second wave feminism, reflecting the wider range of issues it addresses: opposing binaries of sex and gender, promoting sensitivity to intersectionality (an example of which is being all three of female, black, and lesbian), and highlighting the fact that major problems remain, not least domestic violence, rape, and sexual harassment, and the recurrent threat of reproductive rights being rescinded (more conservative states in the US, and European countries under right-wing regimes, like Poland, seek to ban abortion or make access to it more difficult). Problems of race, class, and gender discrimination are still prevalent in developed economies – in some ways sharper because the consciousness that they should not exist throws examples of them into stark relief – and these, together with how society responds to more fluid attitudes to sexual and gender identities, are targets of third wave interest.[30]

With the advent and rapid spread of digital social media a 'fourth wave' or 'digital feminism' – or at least digital activism – is described also, exemplified by 'hashtag' Twitter campaigns such as #MeToo and #SayHerName.

With the evolution and maturation of feminism has come its dispersion into varieties, with resulting conflicts between different wings of the movement. Disagreements between liberal and radical feminists have been mentioned; the differences have theoretical underpinnings. Liberal feminism sought to address inequality and gender injustice through legal reform. Marxist feminists point out that women suffer the double burden of male sexism and capitalist exploitation, supporting the economic arrangements of capitalism with domestic labour which, if it were paid, would be equal to 40 per cent of world GDP. Men control the conditions of work – the nature of the working week, the hierarchies of authority within it, the choice of whom to advance in corporate structures, typically leaving most women below the 'glass ceiling'. Because of these structures women are relegated to part-time, gig, underpaid, low-quality work, and are treated as a dispensable reservoir of spare labour when needed, as in wartime; when men are in the army, women are needed for skilled work in factories; when the men return, the women are laid off.

Radical feminism regards patriarchy as so pervasive in all aspects of society and personal life, and so harmful to women, ranging from demeaning attitudes and language to domestic violence and rape, that for some the remedy is separatism and political lesbianism, and for some of these, in turn, the answer is female supremacy. These are not the only subdivisions; there are also ecofeminism, black feminism, or 'womanism', even 'lipstick feminism' conceived as a way of asserting female autonomy against objectification by owning the objectified image.[31]

These remarks relate exclusively to the feminist movements of developed economic and political societies. The position of the majority of women in the developing world is so far behind that it can only be described as comparable to how things were for women in premodern times. One of the striking features of the women's movements in developed countries is that they have yet to pay more than marginal attention to women elsewhere. Concern about female genital mutilation, forced marriage especially of young girls, and sexual violence against girls and women in India and in places of conflict emphatically should be at the top of human rights and feminist agendas. If feminism in developed countries were to place focus on women in developing and traditional societies, Sustainable Development Goal Five would be closer in reach.

The point can be dramatized by surveying the effect on women of conflict in Africa in the first decade of the twenty-first century. How women are treated when social structures break down is a stark indicator of underlying attitudes. A 2008 *Economist* report on atrocities against women and girls in the Democratic Republic of the Congo read as follows:

All sides – government troops, says the United Nations, as well as the militias – use rape as a weapon of war on a barbarous scale. Most victims, as ever, are women and girls, some no more than toddlers, though men and boys have sometimes been targeted too. Local aid workers and UN reports tell of gang rapes, leaving victims with appalling physical and psychological injuries; rapes committed in front of families or whole communities; male relatives forced at gunpoint to rape their own daughters, mothers or sisters; women used as sex slaves forced to eat excrement or the flesh of murdered relatives. Some women victims have themselves been murdered by bullets fired from a gun barrel shoved into their vagina.[32]

Ann Jones, an aid worker in Liberia, Sierra Leone, and Ivory Coast, published an article in the *Los Angeles Times* entitled 'A War on Women': 'Of all the civilians who suffered, none suffered as disproportionately as women. Today, millions of women in these three West African countries are still struggling to recover; for them, the wars aren't really over at all.' To understand why, consider this description from Amnesty International of the least of the West African wars, the relatively short civil war in Ivory Coast: 'The scale of rape and sexual violence ... in the course of the armed conflict has been largely underestimated. Many women have been gang-raped or have been abducted and reduced to sexual slavery by fighters. Rape has often been accompanied by the beating or torture (including torture of a sexual nature) of the victim ... All armed factions have perpetrated and continue to perpetrate sexual violence with impunity.' An Amnesty International report similarly documented case after case of girls and women, aged 'under 12' to 63, assaulted by armed men.[33]

In another article in the *Los Angeles Times*, United Nations official John Holmes reported:

From the start, sexual violence has been a particularly awful – and shockingly common – feature of the conflict in Congo. Women and girls are particularly vulnerable in this predatory environment, with rape and other forms of sexual abuse committed by all sides on an astonishing scale. Since 2005, more than 32,000 cases of rape and sexual violence have been registered in South Kivu alone. But that's only a fraction of the total; many – perhaps most – attacks go unreported. Victims of rape are held in shame by Congolese society and frequently are ostracized by their families and communities. The ripple effect of these attacks goes far beyond the individual victim, destroying family and community bonds and leaving children orphaned and/or HIV positive.[34]

In a *New York Times* report on the work of a doctor in eastern Congo's Kivu Province the same dreadful story is told:

Every day, 10 new women and girls who have been raped show up at [Dr Denis Mukwege's] hospital. Many have been so sadistically attacked from the inside out, butchered by bayonets and assaulted with chunks of wood, that their reproductive and digestive systems are beyond repair. Eastern Congo is going through another one of its convulsions of violence, and this time it seems that women are being systematically attacked on a scale never before seen here. According to the United Nations, 27,000 sexual assaults were reported in 2006 in South Kivu Province alone, and that may be just a fraction of the total number across the country. Dr Mukwege performs as many as six rape-related surgeries a day. In one town, Shabunda, 70 per cent of the women reported being sexually brutalized. Honorata Barinjibanwa (18), said she was kidnapped from a village during a raid in April and kept as a sex slave until August. Most of that time she was tied to a tree, and she still has rope marks ringing her neck. Her kidnappers would untie her for a few hours each day to gang-rape her, she said.[35]

These horror stories starkly illustrate attitudes to women in their societies, revealing much about their general situation. When the Sustainable Development Goals talk of 'gender equality' the phrase indeed applies to the glass ceilings of the floors below Wall Street board rooms, but in terms of human suffering and need, and in terms of the immense obstacle that gender inequality poses to the health and sanity of humanity overall, it even more importantly applies to women in the developing world.

The purpose of focusing on women's rights and efforts in respect of them, is the point – obvious in one way, but in another way a staggering thought – that *half the human resource* of the planet is undervalued and denied opportunities, either wholly or in part, to contribute their talents and energies. In the US in 2021 women were in the majority, 169.36 million as against 162.06 million men, a majority set to grow. And yet to this day they are still treated as if they are a minority. The phrase 'women, gays and blacks' in rights discourse of the second half of the twentieth century grouped all three from the standpoint of discrimination, but whereas LGBT people and people of African descent are indeed in the minority (the latter in the developed polities of North America and Europe, that is) women are not. As women are half of humanity everywhere the injustice of their situation is commensurately great.

But injustice is injustice whether to many or one. The discrimination suffered by LGBT people, and by African-descended people in countries where they are in the minority, has in each case a long history. Legal disabilities against homosexual men are mainly a modern phenomenon – the first act positively criminalizing gay sex in England was passed in the reign of Henry VIII, but most anti-homosexuality laws in Europe date only from the nineteenth century – and they brought opprobrium with them. Gay rights activism from the 1960s has been successful in institutional terms, as shown by the fact that both the US and the UK legalized same-sex marriage in 2013, homosexual acts between consenting males having been decriminalized in the UK in the 1960s; but acceptance of male gay lifestyles and gays themselves is a metropolitan phenomenon, cities like New York, San Francisco, and London, and earlier examples like Weimar Berlin, being largely welcoming to gay culture, but with distaste and dislike still being common elsewhere in more conservative milieus. Indeed, as already mentioned, in many countries male homosexuality is still a crime, in some of these punishable by death.[36]

Racism and the histories of slavery and colonialism go hand in hand. The tale is too familiar and too tragic to require rehearsing. But it is a mark of the increasing *unacceptability* of racist attitudes and practices that (for a prime example) police violence against African Americans in the US receives the degree of global attention that once – because it was too much a matter of course – it did not. The case of the killing of George Floyd by the policeman Derek Chauvin in Minneapolis on 25 May 2020 illustrates this. It occurred in the full glare of social media, people filming the incident on their cell phones, and the images went viral, fuelling outrage felt by people all over the world. But even incidents that were not filmed – the killings by police of African Americans Daniel Prude, Rayshard Brooks, Breonna Taylor, all in the same year of 2020, with others in the preceding years preserved on the 'Know Their Names' index – have registered with anyone conscious that the time of tolerating racism *de facto* by viewing it as an inevitable feature of the social condition is over.[37]

As with all thinking about how to change attitudes and practices, analysis has to go into detail, from the systemic level in society and organizations to micro-aggressions and unconscious biases displayed even by people who firmly believe themselves not to be racists.

Sustainable Development Goal Sixteen is 'justice'. The foregoing touches on questions of economic justice, gender justice, justice for minorities, all of which can be, and to too great a degree in fact are, absent even when certain other kinds of justice are secure: technical equality before the law (though the expense and tardiness of getting legal remedy is a deep form of practical injustice in itself) and possession of a vote (though unrepresentative electoral systems as in the UK, the US, and India considerably reduce the value of possessing one).[38] The justice sought is recognition and respect for rights. Both concepts – *justice* and *rights* – merit discussion.

Among the virtues standardly extolled in ethical systems, justice stands high. Its importance to the concept of good lives and good societies is universally recognized. Yet its importance in both regards is inversely proportional to its actual presence in the world; as the foregoing shows, ours is a world of so many and such profound inequalities, unfairnesses, social and economic distortions, and outright direct violations of principles both of justice and of rights, that in practice it is as if we scarcely have the concept of justice in our ethical thinking at all.

By 'justice' is meant, at very least, *each having what is due*, where 'each' can mean any of an individual, a group, a state, and

where 'what is due' is any of a range of things – some conten-
tiously included; this is where the debate is hottest – from 'what
is rightfully his/her/their/its own' to 'a fair share' to 'equal
treatment and concern' (which therefore includes not being
discriminated against) to 'protection of his/her/their rights'
and 'fulfilment of his/her/their claims'. As with most large
concepts, its more precise meanings are conditioned by context.
Justice is not the same thing as equality, but is closely related to
equity in the sense of fairness. It is not equality because there
are circumstances where equality would be unjust, as, for example, if an Olympic athlete requiring a daily intake of 5,000 calories and an elderly lady requiring a daily intake of 1,500 calories
were each obliged to consume no more and no fewer than 2,500
calories a day – equal, but unjust. There are plenty of other
circumstances where inequality is unjust, as in the operation of
the laws of a state; every citizen is entitled to equal treatment
before the law, and discriminatory treatment of any kind is
therefore unjust.

But this last remark immediately shows that both the concept
of justice and its application in practical affairs is vexed by
competitions between justice claims. In settings where historically caused disadvantages continue, as – for a prime example –
experienced by African-descended groups in white-majority
countries, one claim of justice supports *positive discrimination* to
compensate for those disadvantages in the interests of a larger
justice. Achieving 'a larger justice' can and typically does require
violation of more immediate and local justice. If a white young
person is denied a place at college so that a young person of
colour – even if on paper less qualified, say – can be admitted,
the former will claim to have been treated unjustly on immediate grounds, while the latter can claim to have been treated justly
on historical grounds; and both will be right.[39]

143

Such circumstances illustrate the familiar point that genuine dilemmas arise when the arguments on both sides are compelling. Which side prevails in such cases is a matter of negotiation, decision, policy, taking into account the larger context and the richer network of interests that need to be served. Positive discrimination in education in a situation of historical disadvantage has much to recommend it. But as with all cases of trade-off, a key consideration concerns the limits to the chosen path. As in times of emergency such as war or global pandemic disease when civil liberties have to be constrained in the interest of security or population health, the constraints should be subject to short-term sunset clauses, and reimposition for a further limited period has, each time, to be deliberate and fully justified by prevailing circumstances. Likewise policies of positive discrimination should be abandoned when they have had their effect; that is obvious. The larger question concerns the subordination of one set of justice claims to another as a structural feature of social and legal arrangements, as happens when an individual is sent to prison for a crime, the injustice of depriving an individual of liberty being of far less moment to society than the justice served by his imprisonment, whatever the aim – whether punishment, rehabilitation, keeping society safe, or some combination of these.

There are many arenas in which injustice and rights-violations are claimed, relating to inequalities within and between societies, poverty, racism, the position of women and gay people, subjection and genocide of minorities, and more. If asked, most people would say that prejudice and the discrimination it causes are fundamentally *unfair*, inequitable, rights-denying; and this makes it important to have a clearer sense of what is involved when such concepts are invoked.

An influential view of justice as fairness was advanced by John Rawls, whose question was: what idea of justice would be accepted as reasonable by any reflective person?[40] He answered it by considering what kind of society people would choose to live in if, before being born, they could do so. Imagine yourself behind a 'veil of ignorance' about what you will be, knowing nothing else about your future – what social class you will occupy; how healthy, intelligent, or talented you will be; what kind of society you will live in. You will only know that basic 'circumstances of justice' will apply, and that the situation will be one of 'moderate scarcity of resources', so that the society's inhabitants' view about what is right will determine the distribution of those resources.

The future citizens of this society, although behind the 'veil of ignorance', will not be entirely without help in making their choice, because they will have a basic idea – what Rawls calls a 'thin conception of the good' – that they would prefer to have more rather than less of a certain range of things which 'it is supposed a rational man wants whatever else he wants', namely, 'rights and liberties, opportunities and powers, income and wealth [and] a sense of one's own worth'. Rawls accordingly argues that people would employ what is known as a 'maximin' strategy for choosing their society, this being a game theory strategy that makes the *most* of the *least* that can be anticipated in a given situation. He argues that people would therefore choose to have the following two principles of justice for their society: first, that each member of society should have an equal right to the greatest degree of basic liberty compatible with everyone else's basic liberty, and second, that inequalities in society should be so arranged that they provide the greatest benefit possible to the least advantaged, and should not prevent offices and positions from being open to everyone under conditions of 'fair equality of opportunity'. The first principle has priority over the second, and 'fair equality of opportunity' has priority over ensuring that the least advantaged have the best deal possible for them in their circumstances.

Rawls' idea that justice is *fairness* envisions a society in which basic organization ensures the kind of distribution of social goods and burdens that thoughtful citizens would find acceptable. He assumes that the society in question is reasonably well-favoured – not wracked by war, drought, disease, or famine. He also assumes that arbitrary advantages – being born into a rich family, or with outstanding talents – do not merit a bigger share of the distribution; the distribution has to be equal unless everyone would benefit from an unequal distribution.

A society would not be just if it ignored the interests of future generations and consumed all its resources selfishly. In the 'original position', therefore, a choice has to be made to agree to a 'just savings' principle, specifying what each generation must conserve for the benefit of successor generations.

The idea of the 'original position' – the position of being behind a veil of ignorance – allows Rawls to describe a set of steps that people would take as they learned more and more about the society they will occupy, moving from general principles to more specific ways of ensuring the greatest possible degree of compatibility between liberty and equality. The aim is to arrive at a *stable* conception of justice that will command agreement because it is 'perspicuous to our reason [and] congruent with our good'.[41]

Rawls' work sparked a great debate; every aspect of his argument has been thoroughly examined – the idea of the 'original position', the problem of differences in natural abilities and starting points as barriers to equality, the two principles of justice he describes, and much more. Take just one – but important – point, the idea of the 'thin conception of the good' that the occupants of the original position need to help them choose what kind of society they want. The veil of ignorance concept is designed to keep the occupants' reflections as impartial as possible, which would be difficult if they knew in advance what their race, sex, or beliefs would be. Their idea of the good has to be 'thin' because if it were 'thickened' by some particular theory of the good – Humanist, Hindu, Muslim, or Christian, for example – then their thinking would be biased by it, and would not automatically command the assent of everyone. But what guarantees that a thin conception will achieve this assent? Recall that it assumes people will desire more rather than less of certain 'primary social goods' which Rawls describes as 'things which it is supposed a rational man wants whatever else he wants ... rights and liberties, opportunities and powers, income and wealth [and] a sense of one's own worth'.[42] Is that right? These are indeed goods highly valued in the mind-set of *liberal individualism*, but to give the people behind the veil of ignorance this theory of what is good begs the question – it in effect specifies in advance the kind of society Rawls thinks they would wish to inhabit; they are being credited with exactly the values that would guarantee that choice.

An allied criticism is that the choosers behind the veil of ignorance are envisaged not merely as equal, but as identical; they are all in the same boat, with the same amount of information, the same thin theory of the good, and the same powers of impartial reason. If you fed a set of computers the same input, one critic remarked, you would get identical outputs; how can an agreement emerge when there is nothing to bargain about?

If we really were behind a veil of ignorance before entering society, our overwhelming consideration would be to protect ourselves as much as possible in case we find ourselves in the most disadvantageous position – for example, being poor, disabled, ill, and alone. This is the reason for Rawls' arguing that arbitrary advantages, such as being born into a wealthy family or having great natural talents, do not justify unequal shares in any distribution, whereas arbitrary *disadvantages* do justify this; and this suggests that the idea of justice and fairness actually come apart; because although it would arguably be *just* that a given person herself should not be arbitrarily deprived of an advantage of birth or talent, it is *fair* to those not thus advantaged to be helped as much as possible when available social goods are being distributed. For example: you meet a rich person with millions of dollars and a poor person with no dollars, and you have ten dollars to give away. Treating them equally by giving them five dollars each would be *just*; giving the ten dollars to the poor person because the rich person already has so much would be *fair*.

A rather more robust, and arguably less humane, view than the one offered by Rawls is put forward in another classic of debate about justice: Robert Nozick's *Anarchy, State, and Utopia*. Rawls' ideas place him in the *liberal* tradition; Nozick's ideas place him in the *libertarian* tradition, a viewpoint further on the right in politics.

Nozick's argument is set out succinctly in the preface to his book. It is that 'Individuals have rights, and there are things no persons or group may do to them (without violating their rights).' The rights are so strong that they place narrow limits on the power of the state in its relation to individual citizens: 'a minimal state, limited to the narrow functions of protection against force, theft, fraud, enforcement of contracts, and so on, is justified; any more extensive state will violate persons' rights not to be forced to do certain things and is unjustified.'[43] This is a classic minimalist 'night watchman' theory of the state.

It follows, Nozick says, that 'the state may not use its coercive apparatus for the purpose of getting some citizens to aid others, or in order to prohibit activities to people for their *own* good or protection.' The libertarian implications of the view lie in this statement. One concerns taxation; taxing people to fund welfare provision is an example of the state coercing its citizens to aid others. Another concerns personal autonomy: laws prohibiting recreational drug use, and laws mandating the wearing of motorbike helmets, are examples of the state deciding what is good for people.

The 'strong rights' Nozick claims individuals have are those of 'the state of nature', much as envisaged in the theories of Locke and Hobbes. These rights predate any social contract or any institutions; they are inviolable, meaning that when some sort of social contract or erection of institutions occurs, these cannot abolish or even limit those rights. Nozick sees individuals as separate persons seeking their own good in their own way, and their separateness as part of the reason why their fundamental rights are inviolable, for they are, in Kant's phrase, 'ends in themselves', and they own themselves and what they do – they have 'property in themselves and their labour'.

Nozick's minimalist state is envisaged as being very like a business corporation, particularly in not financing itself through taxation – perhaps it might get an income by selling its services to citizens, which is one way of interpreting Nozick's 'invisible hand' suggestion that states come into existence in the first place because people band together to protect themselves, a process that eventually gives rise to a dominant protection agency – which is what in effect the state is. This poses a problem for Nozick; why should any form of state come into existence? Anarchists say that states use their monopoly of coercive power to punish those who challenge that monopoly. When the state uses its coercive power to make some people help others, as it does through taxation, it thereby violates their basic rights.

149

Nozick's response is to say what justifies the state's existence, namely the protection it gives its citizens, itself specifies the limits of its powers, because it implies the protection of the citizens from having their rights violated by the protection agency – the state – itself.

The standard criticism of minimalist theories is that they make no provision for *redistributive* justice. Nozick attacks the idea that there is or should be an agency – the state would be the chief candidate – that collects and then equitably shares out social and economic goods. He proposes instead the idea of 'justice in holdings', derived from Locke's idea that in the state of nature people come to own something (something not already in someone else's ownership) by mixing their labour with it. You cut down a tree and chop it into logs for firewood; the firewood is yours; you did the work. This is a 'just acquisition'. Coming to own something by a 'just transfer' – buying it from someone who legitimately owns it and now sells it voluntarily – is another form of just acquisition. A third form is by rectification of past injustices in either acquisition or transfer, as when stolen artworks are restored to their rightful owners, as with victims of Nazism. Coming to own something by any of these three means gives one entitlement to it. If everyone has what he is entitled to, the distribution of holdings in the state is just.

Nozick supports this view with the example of a sportsman who becomes greatly richer than anyone else because everyone else is happy to pay small sums of money to see him play. At the beginning of his career he has the same amount of money as everyone else. Through the course of his career he becomes vastly richer, quite legitimately. An unequal distribution has resulted; is this unjust? Obviously not, Nozick says.

Nozick does not consider acquisition of holdings by inheritance; is that just? The inheritor did not mix his labour with anything to acquire it; the lucky accident of birth is his sole entitlement. It is a matter of decision – social, political – whether acquiring wealth by inheritance is on the same footing as acquiring it by labour from the viewpoint of justice. For there is the question of what difference is subsequently made by starting differences in holdings – the advantages provided in education, opportunities, contacts, access to goods such as health and mobility. And what about natural advantages such as intelligence, good looks, talent – can they be regarded as a kind of holdings violating any idea of entitlement and what follows from it? Is it a consequence of Nozick's view that one can sell one's organs – a kidney, a cornea – or even oneself entirely?

From the point of view of the world's good – redressing the historically-induced disadvantages of racial minorities, respecting the rights of LGBT people, advancing the equality of women – there is something to take from both kinds of theory just described. It might be argued that it is easier to decide upon and apply a concept of justice than a concept of fairness, where the two concepts fall apart, because the former need only engage with adjudications of equality while the latter involves moral judgments requiring independent justification. This is true, but at the same time it is not beyond human competence to debate and decide on the moral priorities suggested by identifiable poverty, hunger, suffering, persecution, and discrimination based on prejudice. Rawls' view provides a guide here; taking as dispassionate and impartial a view as one can about the nature of human experience in the different conditions it can find itself in, tells us much about what we might or even should do when we recognize hunger, suffering, and deprivation; on the most self-regarding basis few people would wish to be so placed themselves, and that tells us much about what we should therefore do in response when we recognize that hunger, suffering, and deprivation are occurring.

It might be surprising to say that Nozick's view has anything to offer the question of rectifying the world's problems, since it seems to be a playbook for the kind of less forgiving version of individualistic capitalism that one sees in the US. But the insistence on inviolable rights strikes a chord. After all, it is the rights of LGBT people, racial minorities, women, and those in the world upon whom the weight of the world's systems most unfairly bears, which are at the centre of questions about global justice and attaining the Sustainable Development Goals. This makes it important, therefore, to consider the question of rights.

The rights possessed by a rights-bearer – a 'rights-bearer' being anything that can be said to have rights of some kind: a human individual, individuals in virtue of a given status or role (children's rights, workers' rights), a people or tribe, a state, animals, a legitimate organization such as a business or club – place an obligation on others to respect those rights. A right is therefore more than a claim; it is an *entitlement*. The key question about rights is what justifies the assertion that they exist.

Thinking about the kinds of rights-bearers just mentioned, it seems that in some cases, such as the rights of a business or club (for example, the right to remedy at law for a crime such as fraud committed against it, or for enforcement of contracts it has entered), the right is conferred by a legislature or a court by a positive decision that such a right exists and must be recognized. But the rights possessed by human beings, such as the rights to life, privacy, and freedom of conscience, are not of that kind, and instead are often said to belong to them purely in virtue of the fact that they are human beings.

'Are often said' – this shows that the question of *natural* rights, rights not positively conferred by a legislative act of some kind, is a contested one. The classic rejection of the idea of natural rights owes itself to the philosopher and legal theorist Jeremy Bentham who regarded talk of natural rights as 'nonsense on stilts' and attacked the French Revolution's 'Declaration of the Rights of Man and the Citizen' in his *Anarchical Fallacies* of 1796. 'Rights are, then, the fruits of law, and of the law alone. There are no rights without law – no rights contrary to law – no rights anterior to the law.'[44] This emphatic rejection of the idea of natural rights goes against a powerful tradition of thought, chief proponents of which included Thomas Hobbes and John Locke, that human beings have always possessed universal, inviolable, imprescriptible, and inalienable rights, and *ipso facto* possessed them before government and law existed, in 'the state of nature' that preceded society.[45] Locke argued that these rights are 'life, liberty and estate (property)'.[46]

An immediate objection to Bentham's view is that there are obvious cases where an enacted law contradicts strong claims to better treatment by someone or something adversely affected by it – think of the Nuremberg Laws against Germany's Jewish population. The ideas of unjust law, immoral law, bad law, get no purchase if enacted law is all there is; and many arguments to the effect that a given law is bad, unjust, or immoral will turn on considerations of the rights that the law in question violates.

At the same time, the appeal to a 'state of nature' in which rights already exist appears on the face of it both arbitrary and weak. The idea of a state of nature is an anthropological fiction – even a troop of baboons has a more elaborate social structure than envisaged for humans in Locke's theory. More likely than not an idea about what a deity might have ordained for humanity in a suppositious Eden is concealed in the notion. What is persuasive in the idea is not the *state of nature* fiction, but considerations about the *nature of human beings* – their capacity to experience pain and pleasure, anxiety and happiness, fear, danger and safety, and their conscious awareness of what can give rise to these experiences not just in the natural but in the social domains they occupy. Many other sentient creatures share these capacities, of course, which is why a case exists for according them the right to be treated in ways that take those facts about them into account. But we regard humans as having hopes and anxieties in relation to these facts which are conscious in character and much greater in extent; they can suffer far more from the violation of their rights than what is immediate and local to the moment of violation itself.

In my view one can cut right through the debate about the origin and justification of rights by taking to heart the lesson taught, most clearly and emphatically, by the circumstances in which the United Nations' Universal Declaration of Human Rights (UDHR) was adopted in 1948. The date is relevant: it is three years after the end of the Second World War, in which appalling atrocities were committed and a mountain of human suffering experienced.

This reveals that *the root of the idea of rights lies in the experience of wrongs.* I offer this as a principle upon which all talk of rights should rest.

The argument for this principle is straightforward. We – we humans – broadly know the kinds of thing that conduce to human flourishing and human suffering; we know that few people like being cold, isolated, hungry, in pain, confined against their will, and denied reasonable opportunities; and that people who do like such things are abnormal. We know that if people have the resources and opportunity to fashion lives for themselves which they regard as good, they have a chance of flourishing. We know why we regard the atrocities and sufferings experienced in the Second World War as

154

atrocities and sufferings. In these perfectly straightforward considerations lies the root of the idea of rights; in them is the source and justification for laying express claim to rights. We identify and institute them by demanding them, reaching for them, and taking a stand on them, on the secure basis of the knowledge – the often bitter knowledge – of the wrongs in which their absence consists.[47]

What is thus claimed includes the right to life, privacy, personal autonomy, freedom of expression, freedom of assembly, freedom of thought, protection by law and due process of law, participation in making decisions affecting one's life and estate, and access to social goods of education and health. The UN Declaration lists twenty-five rights, in Article 29 adding that individuals correlatively have 'duties to the community' without specifying them, but this is an important afterthought nevertheless, because first among those duties is that of recognizing and respecting others' rights.

The flush of enthusiasm that resulted in the unanimous adoption of the UDHR dissipated over the following decades. Lee Kuan Yew of capitalist Singapore and the putatively communist leaders of the People's Republic of China made unconscious common cause in claiming that the idea of human rights is a Western imperialist notion which has little relevance elsewhere – an argument countered by Amartya Sen in pointing out (among other arguments) that Ashoka, the Buddhist ruler of India in the third century BCE, had implicitly recognized the concept in his rulings on intercommunal tolerance.[48] The Organization of Islamic Cooperation issued its Cairo Declaration on Human Rights in Islam in 1990, arguing that aspects of the UDHR are inconsistent with Islam and that all rights listed in the Cairo Declaration are subordinate to Shariah law and the teachings of the Qur'an.

The question to be asked about this repudiation of the universality of human rights is: what is a person living in – for example – China, or in a Muslim-majority country that adopts the Cairo Declaration in place of the Universal Declaration, to be told if they suffer under the kind of situation which elsewhere is covered by the Universal Declaration but in their own circumstances is said not to apply? Consider the examples of a woman obliged against her will to marry this or that stranger, an individual who no longer believes the tenets of his community's religion or who has come to accept those of another religion, an individual whose choices about an educational or career path are denied by the authorities on the grounds that individual rights are subordinate to society's rights and she must serve the state and not herself by working as they instruct her to (sacrificing oneself to 'build communism' for the utopian future was a slogan of the People's Republic of China). These relate to Universal Declaration rights 4, 12, 16, and 18 at least, and arguably others, which respectively protect against being forced into servility (4; forced marriage), the right to a chosen family life (12, 16), and freedom of thought, conscience, and religion (18). What is the case that can be made for saying that violations of these are not wrongs, that ignoring them is justifiable?

In a dispensation which regards significant aspects of the Universal Declaration as inapplicable to its own case, a different evaluation is being given of the kinds of activities from which the Universal Declaration's conceptions of rights, as I argue, arise. So, on that view it is not wrong to force a girl or woman to marry a man she may not know or like. It is not wrong to punish, perhaps even kill, a person for disagreeing with your own religious outlook. It is not wrong to deny people the opportunity to follow their interests and talents in a career of their own choosing. Offering an argument to the effect that these things are not wrong involves offering a defence of what underlies the judgments in question. This matters, because under these judgments lie attitudes that license or in certain circumstances lead to yet greater violations of rights as the Universal Declaration conceives them. If girls and women are items to be disposed in marriage for the services they provide there – domestic labour, child rearing, sex – whatever their own view of the matter, then their feelings and the control they have over their own persons are of much less account than those of men; they are therefore regarded as worth less than men; and it is a short step from there to the horrible treatment so many of them have received at the hands of rapists and abusers in the war-zones of the Congo. The killing of apostates, the imprisonment or execution of gay men, the brutal treatment of African Americans by police, are likewise statements about the relative value of the human life and experience thus being marked down.

In short, refusing to see the suffering or at least inequity caused by the imposition of certain experiences – experiences imposed by social or political choices – as a reason for treating their imposition as a wrong, requires treating some humans as less valuable than others. This in turn requires its own justification. Why is a woman worth less than a man? Why does a man's being gay merit his being put to death? The answers generally lie in traditions and their ancient texts; or in the case of the prescriptive nature of life in a totalitarian regime, in invocation of abstractions like the Nation and the State and its future to whose interests the present and its individual inhabitants must subordinate themselves. Dispassionately viewed, these are rationalizations, not reasons. They do not survive scrutiny. For example: the Judaeo-Christian-Islamic hostility to homosexuality has its roots in the herding past of the Jewish people, for whose ancestors the increase of their flocks of sheep and goats was an existential matter, making it imperative that the seed of the male should go invariably to the egg of the female. Any misdirection of seed (as with Onan in Genesis, 38:7–9) brought the wrath of God. So it came to be an 'abomination for a man to lie with another man as with a woman' (Leviticus, 20:13) and both malefactors should be stoned to death. The world has moved a long way on, and it is no longer acceptable that the anxieties of herders 3,000 years ago should be allowed forcibly to stand in the way of rights to privacy, autonomy, personal life, freedom of belief and conscience. Opponents of a woman's freedom to choose her spouse, or to a gay man's expression of his sexuality, are not themselves being forced to choose a spouse freely or to engage in homosexual acts. It is an unacceptable asymmetry that they should regard it as justifiable to force others in the opposite direction; even more so is the underlying assumption that some people are worth less than others.

The whole point of the Universal Declaration, as its Preamble states, is premised on an assertion of, and thereafter commitment to maintain recognition of, 'the inherent dignity and the equal and inalienable rights of all members of the human family', and the justification implicitly given – that this is 'the foundation of freedom, justice and peace in the world' – required no more demonstration than was given by the circumstances of the Second World War, the ruins of which were still smoking around the newly formed United Nations as it adopted this resolution.

Having the evidence before one's eyes of the reason for asserting that human beings have inalienable rights is one thing; as memories fade and new buildings rise on bomb-sites, moral imagination has to take the place of experience for those who, in peaceful and prosperous parts of the world or high on the social food chain, become not merely blunted to the need for human rights work, but positively inconvenienced by it, as when the

UK government grew impatient with the barrier that the UK's own Human Rights Act posed to deporting terrorism suspects to countries which still have the death penalty. The solution chosen by the UK government was to propose abolishing its own Human Rights Act rather than campaigning for universal abolition of the death penalty.

Another cut-through on the question of human rights and justice is to ask which is more likely to bring realization of the Sustainable Development Goals closer: acceptance and application of the UDHR principles, or acceptance that in some places the rights of women and minorities are less than those of men and majorities?

4

RELATIVISM

What divides people, peoples, and countries? The principal reasons are competing interests, opposing worldviews, and historical enmities themselves a hangover from conflicts caused by either or both of the former. All are familiar features of the world, their multiple expressions filling the news every day.

Competing interests hamper cooperation and motivate arms races, not just arms races involving actual weapons but of every kind, not least – as earlier discussions show – in science and technology. The fear of falling behind in an arms race is a powerful reason for a state (as for a corporation or any competitive group) to continue with the riskiest of developments, and for lying about whether they are pursuing them. Mistrust is endemic to international relations because everyone thinks the same way on this matter, and that is the engine for their believing – knowing – that everyone else is pursuing programmes of research and development as hard and fast as they can. The first part of the self-interest Law, *what can be done will be done*, is self-fulfilling.

The hangover from past conflicts is poison in the waters of international relations. Northern Ireland and the Balkans are obvious cases, but examples are legion from the Middle East to south and east Asia, and persisting undercurrents of dislike manifest themselves in many cases where history has left its stains, as the people of its neighbouring states feel towards Russia, as many Scots feel towards the English, and as many Chinese feel not just for the Japanese but about Westerners – when tensions rise between China and the UK and France the authorities show the film *Huoshao Yuanmingyuan* (Burning of the Summer Palace), and from personal experience I can testify how minatory the popular mood against *waiguoren* (foreigners) becomes.

Past conflicts themselves have their roots in the over-fertile soil of differences in religious and identity commitments, very often the same thing or intimately connected. Here again examples are legion. 'Intercommunal' violence in India may have a number of causes, but at bottom the original dividing line is religion. The same is true of Northern Ireland. There are doubtless atheists on both sides of the Nationalist versus Unionist political divide in that troubled country, and doubtless there are some Catholic Unionists and some Protestant Nationalists, but in the vast majority of cases those atheists will be Catholic-heritage atheists if they are Nationalists and Protestant-heritage atheists if they are Unionists. As a result of religion-segregated schooling the two communities are socially segregated to a significant extent, and in some places their neighbourhoods are separated by walls – called 'peace lines' – that would make a Ming emperor or a Donald Trump proud: five-and-a-half metres (eighteen feet) high, with fortified police stations at various points, running the length of major streets in the capital city Belfast. In 2017 it was announced that under the 'Together: Building a United Community' strategy the 'peace lines' would be dismantled by 2023.[1] At time of writing, one of the consequences of the worst error made by the UK since August 1914, namely Brexit, makes that date look optimistic because it seriously damaged the Good Friday Agreement which had brought peace to that troubled region for nearly a quarter of a century.

These historical divisions are exacerbated when they are associated with war, conquest, and atrocities, and most of them are. Muslims cite the Crusades, the Irish remember their subjugation by English and Scottish Protestants at the time of Cromwell and William of Orange in the seventeenth century, likewise those who fled respectively east and west across the new border between India and Pakistan in August 1947, Armenians remember the repeated genocidal massacres they suffered at the hands of the Turks in 1894–6 and especially 1915–17; all offer examples of the deep and lasting wounds that such events leave. Most borders are drawn in the blood of past conflicts, and that fact alone makes it surprising that there is not even more bitterness in the world, though already overburdened by it.

Differences of religious and identity commitments prompt people to withdraw into a place, physical or psychological, and inscribe a boundary around it – a border, even a wall, for physical places – and hence arise competition, conflict, and perpetuation and deepening of differences by fostering yet sharper such identities. The rhetoric of patriotism, love of country, the sentiment *dulce et decorum est pro patria mori* (it is sweet and proper to die for one's country) – still more: the 'love of God' and service, even martyrdom, for the sake of that God – provide plentiful fuel for this.

If human beings identified themselves primarily and chiefly as human beings, long before they identified themselves by gender, nationality, ethnicity, religion, race, or political affiliation, the artificial causes of rivalry and strife would be fewer, and if these categories did not enter people's heads at all, many of those causes would be non-existent. It is the clash of attitudes, outlooks, belief systems, all held deeply enough to generate a sense of significant difference and therefore suspicion and even hostility towards those who do not share them, which is the problem: 'our way is right, yours is wrong', 'we have the truth, you live a lie'.

There are broadly three ways in which such differences of outlook can be overcome. One is by coercion, as when you conquer those who disagree with you and force them to accept your way of looking at things. The second is enlightened self-interest, in which you seek mutual toleration and *convivencia*, a term used by historians to describe the basis for coexistence among Muslims, Jews, and Christians in the Iberian peninsula between the ninth and fifteenth centuries CE.[2] The third is some form of altruism, ranging from willing conversion to the others' viewpoint in order to keep the peace, or assuring them of the superiority either of their persons or their viewpoint even if you do not go wholly over to it – or at any rate in some way yielding sufficiently to ensure that the *amour propre* of the others is kept in good order.

Coercion was frequently the method of choice in history. It did not always have to be at the point of the sword; most people are pragmatic enough, generally speaking, to recognize when the third 'altruistic' route is the wisest option, so the mere presence or even promise of a conquering army can be a fruitful motive to that end. An example of the point-of-a-sword strategy is what happened after the Battle of the White Mountain outside Prague in 1619, when the Catholic army of Duke Maximilian of Bavaria beat the Protestant army of the 'Winter King' Frederick IV of the Palatine. The Catholic army brought Bohemia and Moravia back to the Catholic faith by a series of atrocities – some of them witnessed, but never thereafter mentioned, by the philosopher René Descartes who was with the Catholic troops.[3] The conquests by Muslims of Arabia, Persia, North Africa, and

Iberia in the seventh to ninth centuries CE was effected by a mixture of military and other means, mainly military to begin with – relatively easily because the Persian and Byzantine empires were exhausted and depleted after fighting long wars against each other – but thereafter by more peaceful conversion as Islam proliferated along trade routes. As a faith both simple to understand and practise, and pragmatically convenient to accept given that its votaries were in power, establishing itself was also relatively easily done.

Tolerance has succeeded in restoring and thereafter keeping the peace in most parts of Christendom since the terrible Reformation-sparked violence of the sixteenth and seventeenth centuries. Religion was never the sole motive of those conflicts, but it was the major one. In the Thirty Years' War of 1618–48, fought mainly between the Catholic Holy Roman Empire and various of its constituent and neighbouring Protestant states, the desire to repossess lost territory and its revenues was of course an inducement, alongside the persuasive argument put to Emperor Ferdinand II by his Jesuit confessor, Wilhelm Lamormaini, that restoring the Catholic faith would ensure his place in heaven. Likewise, France's Wars of Religion of 1562–98, remarkable for their religious bitterness, were about power as well as faith; Henri IV converted from Protestantism to Catholicism to placate his Catholic rivals and secure the French crown – *Paris vaut bien une messe* (Paris is well worth a mass) he said. In the Thirty Years' War intolerance was a mark of the conflicts; wherever Catholic troops reconquered a Protestant area, the belief that Protestantism was satanically inspired gave the officers of the Inquisition, who followed the troops everywhere, grounds to instigate witch hunts and trials.[4] Witch-hunting had become increasingly prevalent in Europe in the preceding century, inflamed by the new religious differences, and was at last extinguished in the eighteenth-century Enlightenment; but while it lasted it was both a murderous symptom of intolerance and diagnostic of intolerance's sources: fear, misunderstanding, ignorance, the spurring of hostility by the politics of identity.

Exhausted by the struggles, Europe and the places to which its imperial adventures spread Christianity at last accepted that *convivencia* is the best option, and with the exception of places like Northern Ireland (and parts of Scotland; even the football clubs Rangers and Celtic in Glasgow, respectively Protestant and Catholic, and Heart of Midlothian and Hibernian in Edinburgh, likewise respectively, cleave to the confessional divide)[5] this is generally though not completely the case. It is quite common for Protestants to be hostile to Catholics, whose Mariolatry, vast pantheon of saints, superstitious practices, subservience (historically) to priests and nuns, and saccharine iconography appear repellent, while to Catholics the sterile aesthetic and joyless excesses of puritanism in some versions of Protestantism are equally unpalatable. The Protestant 'ascendancy' in Ireland looked haughtily down on the Catholic Irish as no better than ignorant peasants stupefied by their religion – uncomprehending of the Latin and choked by the fumes of incense in church, terrified of hell, servile to their priests, but sinning unstoppably in the paradoxical confidence that confession would absolve them or at least shorten their time in purgatory, they seemed altogether contemptible.

Tolerance of those whom you think contemptible is an insulting form of condescension. This is even so with tolerance of those you think are merely misguided in their beliefs, but you indulge them anyway. It is a belittling and demeaning attitude. For this reason the concept of tolerance is itself in bad odour. In the 'woke' culture of the twenty-first century's first quarter, tolerance is not enough; one has to *respect* others' views. It is vastly easier to do this, or say that you do, if you do not hold your own views very strongly. A lukewarm or unreflective Christian can be accommodating to a Muslim, Hindu, or Jew by being satisfied with a vague notion that everyone worships the same God in the end. As members of an absolute minority everywhere other than the state of Israel itself, with a worldwide population in 2019 of just 14.7 million, Jews are perforce tolerant of other faiths. Muslims are the least generally tolerant, on the grounds that they take non-Muslims – infidels, *kafirs* – to be dangerously mistaken in refusing to hear the message of their prophet.

A focal case of the intolerant religious mind-set is easy to describe. If you think that someone else is wrong in his religious beliefs, to tolerate him and his religion in your midst is tantamount to abetting the wrongness. If you think he poses a danger to your own faith and its adherents, you are putting them at risk by tolerating him. If you think he is misled by the devil, you are doing the devil's work by letting him continue to manifest his faith. In the days of the Inquisition in fifteenth-century Europe it was sincerely believed that to kill a heretic was to do him a favour – by diminishing the length of time he languished in his heresy, you were shortening the length of his sufferings in purgatory. At the same time you were protecting the faithful from being misled and seduced by him into the same heresy. This argument – that killing was a kindness – does not accord with some of the tortures and execution methods employed.

Examples abound today of religious intolerance, intolerance by secular authorities towards religious groups, and intolerance of ethnic minorities. Muslim minorities in China and Myanmar – the Uighurs of Xinjiang and the Rohingyas of Rakhine respectively – are actively persecuted. Hindu intolerance of Muslims in India frequently causes outbursts of intercommunal conflict. Mutual intolerance among Muslim sects, and Muslim intolerance of non-Muslims, especially when the latter asperse Islam or Muhammad, not infrequently take violent forms.

One test case for *convivencia* is anywhere Muslim immigrant minorities live. Europe's wealth and opportunities have been a major draw for people from Muslim-majority countries, with the result that significant communities of Muslims live in Germany, France, the Netherlands, and the UK. On the whole, the host communities have accepted and tolerated Muslim immigrants from the religious point of view, so that when trouble occurs it is primarily on race or ethnic grounds. This is because most European countries are functionally secular, and *avid* devotees of one or another Christian sect are few in number, so questions of theology are not uppermost in the minds of the host population. The reverse is true for the Muslim immigrants, many of whom are extremely sensitive to real or perceived insults to their faith and their prophet. An unhelpful feedback mechanism sets to work; Muslims' own vehemence stimulates hostility towards them; they refuse to accept that others do not share their sensitivities, and try to punish them or coerce them to do so – the Charlie Hebdo murders in Paris in January 2015, like the outcry prompted by the cartoons in the Danish newspaper *Jyllands-Posten* in September 2005, are cases in point. What Muslims may see but do not accept is that it is a key feature of European culture that criticism, even ridicule, of the positions people take, and the beliefs they hold, is a precious and important structural feature of the liberal Enlightenment settlement that followed on rejection of absolute monarchy and totalitarian ideology (which then meant religion) in the eighteenth century. Nazi and Soviet attempts to reintroduce a secular form of totalitarian ideology were opposed and defeated in the twentieth century, the first within fifteen years and the second (thinking of the post-1945 Cold War) in forty-five years. As in effect a totalizing religion, dominating every aspect of Muslims' lives everywhere and most aspects of society in Muslim-majority countries, Islam is viewed as hegemonic and illiberal, so its attacks on the anti-hegemonic and liberal sensibility of the West are regarded by many Westerners with hostility.

Evidently, the opposition of sensibilities involved is an unhealthy one from the point of view of the world's peace and stability, and diminish the prospects of cooperation in dealing with global problems.

One essential for a more peaceful and cooperative world is that members of any given group have to learn to accept that those they define as members of out-groups do not share their views and values, and that they cannot force, by violence or any other means, compliance with their wishes about how others should behave. Muslims legitimately expect non-Muslim visitors to their countries to take account of cultural sensibilities there. They also rightly expect to be able to practise their faith wherever they are – in whatever country, no matter what its cultural background or what religion its majority population practises. That should include recognizing that in Western countries matters of ideology – politics, religion – and cultural choices are fair game for criticism and satire. The Western view is more or less this: that one does not discriminate against or make fun of people on grounds of age, sex, sexuality, gender, disability, and ethnicity – things that are not a matter of choice, excepting the possibilities of sex and gender change. But matters of choice – of which religion is one, however hard it might be to shed the outlook one was inculcated into as a child, or which might involve ostracism from one's community if one leaves it – are fair game. After all, all religions are ridiculous from *some* point of view, for however devout one is in one's own faith, from its perspective the tenets and practices of other faiths cannot all seem, let alone be, justified and appropriate.

The aim of these remarks is to reintroduce the notion of tolerance in a new key – perhaps by adjusting the term itself to echo John Locke's celebrated writings on the subject, which helped to bring internal peace to the very 'broad church' of the Church of England, where tastes in styles of worship and liturgy ranged from austere puritan observance to sumptuous High Church ritual reminiscent of the Roman rite. This term is *toleration*. If it were defined as the recognition of a secure space that another value system can occupy in return for having one's own secure space, it would capture the *convivencia* objective that a globalized world, inhabited cheek-by-jowl by a variety of value systems, must seek. At the same time, toleration thus conceived requires agreeing on certain fundamentals; and identifying these requires reflecting on what is meant by views about relativism – more on this later.

But first it is important to remark that offence is never a justification for violence. Ordinary courtesy should restrain people from insulting or offending people gratuitously, which is one side of the equation. On the other side, knowing when humour is humour, and accepting that others see one differently from how one sees oneself, is a mark of maturity. A religion that infantilizes its followers so that they cannot be grown-up in dealing with differences of view is not serving its members well. Understanding *toleration* as the positive work of achieving *convivencia* – the ability to live together peacefully – for mutually beneficial ends, rather than 'tolerance' as a condescending attitude that demeans by implication as it indulges, is to make the effort to adjust the key in which talk of mutual tolerance is conducted; it is to try to reintroduce an important concept which recognizes differences of belief and outlook but insists on a mutual provision of space so that both can exist.

If the way people think about the world is conditioned by their history and culture, it is not surprising that they might arrive at a variety of different, even incommensurable, perspectives. Noting that different ways of thinking about the world exist but rejecting the idea that some ways of doing this are better, more accurate, or more morally acceptable than others, is *relativism*.

A distinction is sometimes drawn between cultural relativism and cognitive relativism.[6] The former concerns the differences between different contemporaneous belief and value systems, and between different historical phases of the same system within a given culture. Cognitive relativism – if such a thing exists in the way about to be described – concerns putative differences between the way different groups of human beings experience the world in the most basic perceptual ways. The idea here is that at the neuropsychological level of acts of seeing and hearing, the targets of these acts are perception-independent, reidentifiable, and individually discriminable objects or events, occupying space and time, interacting causally, and bearing properties of various kinds, and that this is so just in virtue of the way a human being's sensory pathways are configured in her body and brain. The problem with this latter notion is that there is no culturally detachable way to talk of seeing and hearing except as *seeing-as* and *hearing-as* – that is, as acts which are soaked through with interpretation, this in turn being a function of cultural conditioning.

If there is no such thing as cognitive relativism, then perhaps there is really no such thing as relativism at all. For it would seem, on the face of it, that cultural relativism is not really relativism either, because our ability to recognize that another culture, or an earlier phase of our own culture, is different in identifiable respects, turns on our being able to *recognize* the differences as differences; which means that there must be enough in common between our own and the other culture to permit mutual access and understanding. But if such access is possible, it must be because there are some fundamental things that are shared; and if there are such things, then the differences are superficial and, as it were, intertranslatable.

But it is precisely this point which is denied by advocates of relativism. They argue that the appearance of mutual accessibility is misleading, because far from gaining entry to the other scheme we are merely reinterpreting it into, or 'reading-in', the categories of our own scheme. And this is the best we can hope to do, they say, because to grasp how subscribers to another scheme understand things, we need to translate their language into our own, and translation is only ever approximate; it is not possible to make it fully determinate. Relativists do not of course mean the empirically false thesis that there are languages which cannot be translated (certain *scripts* might not yet be translated, like Minoan Linear A; but that is not the same thing); they mean the philosophical thesis that we can never be sure which out of alternative translations most accurately captures the meaning of the discourse we are trying to translate.

The arena in which relativism is most challenging is morality. A moral relativist holds that what is regarded as good and bad, right and wrong, depends on the *situation* – this being a richly freighted term denoting a whole matrix of cultural, historical, and sectional positioning – of the person making the relevant judgment, so if people occupying different moral standpoints disagree about whether some action or situation is good, each is entitled to her view and there is no way of adjudicating between them.

This view premises the claim that moral value is not an objective feature of the world. If it were, then if two or more people disagree about what is good, only one of them can be right. Much ordinary moral thinking wavers between this view and various forms of relativism of a subjectivist kind; for example, those saying that our moral judgments arise from our emotional responses or from the historical and geographical accident of our personal cultural origins. Anyone holding a version of a subjectivist view would find it hard, to say the least, to claim that his moral outlook is right and that competing views are wrong. An example of an objectivist view, by contrast, is religion; although one's religion is almost always a product of what one's parents' religion was, and of where and when one was born – just the same factors as the subjectivist cites as justifying moral relativism – one is nevertheless committed to believing that one's religion's morality is correct, and differing moralities therefore wrong.

In this confusing landscape it is important to distinguish between the anthropological – empirical – observation that as a matter of fact different cultures might have different value systems, and the relativist's claim that different value systems are of equal merit. The former, empirical, observation is of course unexceptionable; the latter philosophical claim is contentious, and for moral objectivists unacceptable.

The objectivist position appears harder to sustain than the relativist one. The relativist says that the basis of moral judgments is the traditions and experience of a community, so that when they take a given moral principle to be true, they have resources for justifying the claim in their beliefs and traditions. This can look compelling in some cases. To take just one example, that of polygamy, one notes that some societies regard it as unexceptionable and even good, others as unacceptable and bad, and in each case it is the beliefs and traditions that provide the justification.

But then one considers the objectivist's claim that some things – torture of children, murder, rape, military aggression, theft, unkindness, and cruelty – are wrong everywhere, anywhere, for anyone, in any culture or society. This is a claim to the universality of fundamental moral values, and its denial requires not that there be differences of opinion of what *counts* as (say) cruelty or rape, but whether *agreed instances* of cruelty and rape can ever be right in one system of values while wrong in others.

A suggestion that seeks to reconcile the objectivist and rela-tivist position might be that value systems are a mixture of both universal and parochial features. On this view, there are some universal moral truths, and there are some moral tenets that are more variably a matter of tradition and custom, such as polygamy or the age of sexual consent. Another idea is that fundamental truths are the same everywhere but how they are acted upon differs; in one society adult offspring might honour their ageing parents by buying them a bungalow at the seaside, while in another the adult offspring might honour their ageing parents by eating them. The principle – honour thy mother and thy father – is observed in both, though in radically differ-ent ways.

Relativism is a natural corollary, perhaps indeed it is the defining characteristic, of postmodernism. A commendable motivation for it is the desire to promote reciprocal respect between different cultures and value systems, and to make amends for cultural as well as other imperialisms of the past. The price paid for this worthwhile motive is a lack of guide-rails for dealing with the very real problems faced by the world and people in it.

There is a cut-through on this question of values. It is to cite again the fundamental justification for thinking about human rights – that there are certain fundamental experiences that human beings can have and which the vast majority of them do not like, such as being hungry, in pain, cold, alone, abused, oppressed, imprisoned, denied opportunities, treated as worth less than some other group or gender, and the like. Aversion to these conditions is natural, and there are good reasons for it: they are unpleasant at least, but even more so they are harmful and, when extreme, dangerous to sanity and to life. Our ability to recognize that someone is suffering in one or more of these ways is a natural fact likewise, and it speaks to us about something that can be done – that we can do – in response. Consider the fact that a sadist is one who recognizes suffering but enjoys it and even enjoys inflicting it; this is a perversion of the standard reaction that people have in witnessing suffering, which is sympathy or concern. In these simple and pervasive facts lies the root both of moral sensibility and of the justification for human rights claims. And here therefore is a striking realization: that the concept of human rights *just is* the concept of a universal objective morality – universal and objective because it is anchored in facts about the human central nervous system, both its capacity for suffering and its capacity for recognizing and responding to that suffering.

This puts things in the negative register, concerning *suffering*, the response to it, the measures to prevent it occurring. This case makes itself. There is more resistance to the idea of the positive case – that knowing what conduces to human *flourishing*, we should aim to produce it and share it. The argument for this is no different for the argument in the negative register: we know in general what makes for flourishing – security (freedom from fear or anxiety), education, health, resources to hand for making or taking opportunities. These are hardly outrageous demands. They are the least any of us would wish for ourselves and those we care about. Again, the point can be offered to the most callous self-interest: a world in which these positive helps are available to all is a world safer, healthier, and wealthier than one where they are at best only patchily available, so that hundreds of millions of people are without them, people whose presence on the planet in that condition is a drain on it and a potential threat to it.

This discussion touches on the hardest of the moves people have to make in order to face the world's problems. This is the move to toleration, as defined earlier. And the basis for the implicit contract that allows the recognition of the other's secure space – 'good fences make good neighbours' – is acceptance of the following principle in regard to rights: that *pending a resolution of differences over what should be included in any list of human rights, one recognizes that the positive rights claimed by the other party must be accommodated as far as possible.* One might not seek them for oneself or one's own; one might argue against them, or try to persuade the other to change them, to drop them, or to adopt what one regards as better ones; but pending the outcome of such discussion, the least required for mutual toleration is acceptance that the other is going to live by the commitment he has made to his rights.

This is the hardest move because it is uncomfortable for both sides. For example: a European liberal is going to have to accept some uncongenial facts about the situation (using this in the technical sense described earlier) she would have to share with her sisters in a Muslim-majority country if she chooses to live there. A Muslim living in France or England is going to have to accept that people in the host culture make satirical and sometimes outrageous jokes about religion.

It is obvious how this suggestion breaks down when one pushes it to a dramatic contrast. Consider a supposed trade-off between the liberal West recognizing the right of certain societies to practise female genital mutilation (FGM) in return for being able to satirize religious ideas and figures without being murdered. The idea of a mutual recognition of contrasting rights is the idea of accepting this trade-off, at least pending further progress towards a consensus on values. To a Western sensibility the lack of any moral equivalence between a horrendous crime against girls and women and satirizing a religious figure puts this debate out of the park. It is incomprehensible how tens of thousands of people can want to kill someone for printing satirical cartoons, while themselves condoning or at least tolerating the practice of FGM. I have to confess to finding this incomprehensible myself. But an associated practical point is of moment here. News that FGM is practised on girls in Britain did not result in the murder of anyone associated with the practice, or demonstrations threatening violence against societies in which FGM is practised. Angry and appalled voices were raised in protest, and it was outlawed in the UK in 1985. So we do not accept FGM here, and we campaign against it happening anywhere. But we do not riot and murder as a way of expressing moral disgust at it. Countries where FGM is part of tradition or religious observance doubtless outlaw publications satirizing religion and religious figures.[7] But at present anyway the risk anyone runs of doing this, even in his own country, is the risk of being murdered. The moral equivalence being sought is not between FGM and satire, but between the sharply contrasting ways in which opposition to them is respectively expressed.

It would be an advantage to be able to say that although people in the liberal West deplore certain fundamentalist religious regimes denying education to girls, we do not send armies to invade them in response. Alas, though the US-led invasion of Afghanistan in 2001 was not about restoring girls' right to an education, the complex of causes on both sides leading to that intervention was of a piece with sentiments about that kind of matter on both sides. The liberal West does not have a secure grip on the moral high ground, though fundamentalists' grip on the low ground of coercion and denial of rights is indeed secure. But the fact that everyone can jab accusatory fingers at everyone else does nothing to help the central cause at issue: finding ways for everyone to cooperate in dealing with what are problems for everyone. If one thing is universal – embracing and involving and including everyone – in the threats we face, it is the threats themselves.

5

THE SOLUTION

There are two general ways in which the global problems described in this book will end. One is by the concerted and cooperative action of humanity preventing, mitigating, or managing them well enough. The other is by reality forcing itself on humanity when the problems are beyond humanity's capacity to deal with them. In this latter case the end of the problems could, in the extreme, include the end of humanity; but even a best-case outcome for reality's way of dealing with any or all of climate catastrophe, runaway technology, uncontrolled genetic mutations, upheavals prompted by injustices that can no longer be tolerated by those who suffer them, will not be pretty.[1] This is the future we are currently set to bequeath to our children and grandchildren if we fail to have the plain good sense to deal with them, rationally and morally, now.

There are, to repeat, principally two barriers to a united endeavour by humankind. One is conflict and competition that keeps 'arms races' going in economic and technological spheres. The other is ideological differences (political, religious, cultural) which keep people, peoples, and states apart, suspicion and hostility a common feature of the mutual perceptions underwriting the standoffs involved. Neither barrier is insurmountable.

There are many international organizations such as the UN and WHO, and many examples of successful international cooperations that ignore all the adventitious differences between people and states, such as the Sustainable Trade Initiative, the World Resources Institute, C40 Cities, the International Finance Corporation, the Large Hadron Collider project at CERN, and others, which prove that differences can indeed be overcome, and are irrelevant in the face of larger and more important common interests. Indeed, one might cite any wartime alliance as a model; in the face of great threat, local reasons for quarrels become irrelevant.

And yet the existential crises facing humanity have yet to bring the world together as it does at CERN and the WHO. Instead, we see continued wrangling and suspicion that so hamper the effort at joint action, with nations and politicians behaving like sailors squabbling on the bridge of a ship as it sails, at increasing speed, towards an iceberg.

Note that the first kind of barrier – the 'arms race' barrier; the fear of falling behind in economic and technological competition – is an instance chiefly of the first part of the self-interest Law, *what can be done will be done if it serves the interests of those who can do it.* The second kind of barrier – ideology that makes some things stick in the throat so much that one cannot bring oneself to do it or allow it (tolerating homosexuality in a Muslim-majority country, for example) – is an instance chiefly of the second part of the Law, *what can be done will not be done if it is unacceptable to those who can stop it.* In practice, of course, both aspects of the Law apply in both cases; one can rephrase matters to fit either formulation, but putting it this way is illuminating.

Again to repeat: the first kind of barrier arises from the imperative to protect interests. A government can say it wishes to maintain economic growth for the benefit of its populace, and for that

reason be less than whole-hearted about measures that will interfere with growth, such as limiting emissions while it is reliant on
fossil fuels for energy. The second kind of barrier arises from the
imperatives of identity and belief. Nationalism and religious
commitment are chief examples. Take the barrier erected by religion: if you are a devotee of a particular faith, your belief in its
truth is simultaneously a belief that other religions are wrong in
important respects, indeed may even be evil. How can you tolerate them? If on these grounds you can hinder cooperation requiring concessions to another religious community, you therefore
will. This presents itself as an immovable obstacle.

The imperatives in both cases are artificial. The first lies, in
significant part, in the ambition of politicians to remain in
government by satisfying the populace economically, thereby
improving their chances of re-election, or (in non-democracies)
of retaining control by keeping the populace quiescent enough.
The second lies in the promotion of nationalistic or religious
emotions by leaders whose influence or power depends on
doing so; demagogues, preachers, imams.

There is a general solution to the world's problems, a solution
that would overcome the immense barrier of the self-interest
Law and not merely end the problems but provide for improvement, peace, security, and shared prosperity across the board. It
is a utopian solution; it is unlikely to happen in anything like this
form, at least until the far side of a general catastrophe has
occurred, if one does occur and humanity survives it. It is therefore a dream solution, not a real one. But it is appropriate to
contemplate the ideal, because it sets a horizon to strive towards;
the closer one can get to it, the better.

This ideal – this *idealized* – solution is the obvious one: it is
for peoples and their governments around the world to act selflessly in concert to address the difficulties and to share the

resources, the endeavour, the burdens and benefits, that follow. To get governments around the world to do this, or at least those which are the major players in harming the environment and pushing the development of dangerous technologies, they need to be appointed by and accountable to populations who are well-informed, judicious, long-term in their thinking, and altruistic. In a perfected state of affairs all communities would be democracies consisting of people like this, and the governments they form would accordingly act not in the interests of partisan political agendas and ideologies, but in the interests of the rationally and dispassionately evaluated welfare of the planet and of all its occupants (all species and environments according to their natures). In the case of human beings, the socioeconomic arrangements would be premised on the fact that they flourish most when healthy, educated, well-resourced, and secure, with worthwhile endeavours to engage their talents and energies, thus bringing satisfaction and a sense of value to life. In the case of the rest of the planet's inhabitants – plant and animal alike – undisturbed and unpolluted habitats are the necessary conditions of their flourishing.

In this ideal scenario, there would be concerted action on climate; there would be moratoria on technological developments until all their implications are well understood and good regimes of management of them have been devised; and injustices would be remedied and respect for rights of individuals and peoples enshrined and enforceable in the constitutions of all states.

Achieving any of these desiderata has so far proved impossible; indeed the opposite is the norm. But this at least gives us a clear idea of the ideal.

It is not just politicians and preachers who are the problem; far from it. Large sections of populations, indeed in many cases majorities, are not interested in the ideal scenario, at least when it comes down to hard practice. Short-term interests and emotional sticking-points are powerful in their effects. A second-best solution, accordingly, is for governments to act as above, even if it has to be in the face of dissent from some, many, or all of their populations. This would amount to benign dictatorship, and it controverts every principle of democracy that the best in humanity have worked to create since the dawn of the Enlightenment. A defender of this muscular solution might say that those who have striven for government appointed by informed and responsible populations have ever been in a minority, persistently defeated by the short-termism and self-interest of pluralities, to which political factions therefore pander in order to gain power, and which they have to keep feeding with the equivalent of bread and circuses in order to stay in power. It is this combination – the self-interested people and the short-termist governments they produce – that makes the self-interest Law such an iron law.

There are of course dictatorships in the world, but in an over-all state of the world in which economic and military competitions are the main drivers of the choices governments make, there is no practical difference, from the point of view of the world's welfare, between them and putative democracies. In this respect they are as ineffective as each other. And this leaves aside the objectionable nature of dictatorship as a form of government itself.

Unless we think that we might as well let the various developing threats overwhelm the world in its present state, so that from the aftermath – the wreckage – a new and different order can be built by the survivors, we are obliged to look for less than ideal solutions or at least palliatives. As intimated in the Introduction, these require a case-by-case approach, appropriate to climate, technology, and justice issues on their own terms; but a concerted solution is required so that the right kinds of international cooperation can be relied upon in each – a global determination to work out the particular solutions together.

The easiest is the most urgent: the climate challenge. International efforts have identified what needs to be done, and international agreements have been signed to do them. The climate conferences of Kyoto (1997), Paris (2016), and Glasgow (2021) are landmarks in the process. But at least three things disturb this optimistic picture. One is its vulnerability to political factors such as changes of government; another is shifts in public opinion; a third is fluctuations in international tensions. Any of these can put international efforts under strain, or upset them altogether. As an example of the first: the four unhappy years of the Trump presidency in the United States were a setback for efforts to deal with the climate emergency. As an example of the second: some forms of climate activism can alienate public sentiment and provide opportunities for delayers or deniers to get a platform.[2] As an example of the third: progress is hampered by chronic disagreements among the major international players – the US, China, Russia, and the EU – and among them and other significant states (chiefly India and Japan) over other important issues. China's military penetration into the Spratly Islands is a provocation; criticism of its extremely poor human rights record in Tibet and Xinjiang is a barrier to better relations with the US and the EU; its tensions with India and Japan and its support of North Korea make it an uncongenial partner in international efforts; its threat to the independence of Taiwan is perennial. Russia's irredentism on its western and southern borders, not least in relation to the Ukraine and Georgia, likewise keep international relations uneasy, as does its habit of sending agents to murder exiled Russian dissidents abroad. Local and short-term interests of political cliques such as the far right of the Republican Party in the US and the Brexiters in the UK – the latter exploiting the atrophied condition of the country's constitutional arrangements, which make capture of government on minority support a commonplace – are destabilizing not only internally but in respect of relations with neighbours, allies, and competitors.

The other two areas of difficulty – technological developments in AI, weapons, and genetics, and deficits of justice and rights – are far more complex because they are internally disparate and much of the public knowledge of them, where it exists, is too often simplistic and alarmist in character, the latter fact itself a cause of indifference and scepticism because scare stories have the effect of turning attention off rather than heightening awareness. What they share with the climate question is the urgent need for sound widespread public knowledge of what is happening and what is at stake. The climate question is ahead in this respect, not enough and only after a huge struggle to get people to notice; but it is ahead. Unlike the climate question whose worst-case prospects are well understood, the consequences of runaway technologies are unpredictable – one need only consider AGI; a machine intelligence that created itself is not something whose outlook, intentions, and behaviour one can predict.

Likewise, it is an open question what the values and aims of genetically modified future people, or a diverging new subspecies of genetically superior people, will be. Perhaps this is the least of our worries, given that we will not be around to benefit or suffer from whatever the differences are; but the thought that our children and grandchildren could be like us in sharing our sentiments and values, but be living in a world alongside one or more of AGI, autonomous weapons systems, a degraded environment, and genetic mutants of other species including pathogens, should at very least give us pause.

In the three decades following the Second World War, with the ghastly evidence of division and conflict fresh in most minds – the clean-up was still in process: bomb sites remained in my neighbourhood of London into the 1970s and beyond – there was a general tendency across the world for countries to come together, to work together, to form international groupings. The European Economic Community was formed; the Cold War principles of the Warsaw Pact and NATO were defensive alliances but in practical terms cooperated on much besides; the Non-Aligned Movement founded at the Bandung Conference of 1955 was – despite the name – an alignment of developing countries seeking to stay out of the Cold War; for a time the Soviet Union and China made common cause as nominally communist states. At the supra-international level the UN and its organs such as the Human Rights Commission were formed. Other international organizations of lesser geographical scope came into existence, such as the OECD (Organisation for Economic Co-operation and Development) and the CSCE (Conference on Security and Co-operation in Europe; founded in 1975 on the Helsinki Accords it became the OSCE, Organization for Security and Co-operation in Europe, in 1995). The states of south-east Asia formed ASEAN (Association of Southeast Asian Nations), African states formed the AU (African Union), South American states formed MERCOSUR (Mercado Común del Sur), all reflecting the wisdom of seeking closer cooperation with near neighbours and trading partners in imitation of the European Union. It was as part of this general movement to cooperation and cohesion that the UK, under a Conservative government, joined the EEC in 1973. The motive was not chiefly idealistic, but practical; the UK economy was in chronic and worsening trouble, and membership of the EEC and subsequent EU rescued it in the decades that followed. On the other hand, it could be argued that, likewise, the aim of preventing bad consequences of global warming and unmanaged technological change is wholly practical and needs little idealism, only common sense.

But these centripetal forces have become centrifugal in some respects, as indicated by the Brexit phenomenon and the Trump Mexico wall – more a symbolic than a practical measure; no border wall ever kept anyone in or out of anywhere permanently, as Hadrian's Wall, the Great Wall of China, and the Berlin Wall amply testify. But it is an unpromising development nevertheless, from the viewpoint of the need for yet greater cooperation than the post-1945 centripetalism achieved. Hope is kept alive by determined and imaginative people and organizations. Climate change conferences continue (the latest being the UN climate summit conference – UNFCCC or COP26 – in Glasgow in November 2021) despite continued undershooting of targets already set, and at time of writing there are proposals for a fiftieth anniversary conference in Finland to mark the Helsinki Accords of 1975 to which non-members China, Russia, and the US are to be invited, to discuss the climate, the Arctic (with sea-ice disappearing, sea routes and resources exploration prospects are opening there), and military tensions relating to the South China Sea, Taiwan, the Sino-Indian border regions, and elsewhere.[3]

So far, these remarks make the prospects of solutions to the world's crises – in their joint effect: crisis – look dim. Getting as close as possible to the ideal solution described earlier is hard, and it is complicated by the point iterated several times, that each arena of crisis – climate, technology, justice – requires its own targeted set of endeavours. But the fact that it is hard is no reason not to try. Indeed, there is no option but to try; as follows.

The ideal solution described earlier requires – as noted – that peoples and their governments act, selflessly and jointly, to address the difficulties and to share the resources, the endeavour, the burdens and benefits. So, *people have to understand clearly what the problems are, and be motivated to act accordingly, chiefly by obliging their primary instrument – their governments – to act in concert with other governments to take the necessary steps.* No doubt anyone who has tried to encourage 'people to understand clearly what the problems are' will utter a horse-laugh at this assertion; strenuous efforts have been made for years to wake up populations around the world to the fact that they are in a bus racing towards a cliff-edge, with far too little effect as yet. True. But there is no option; those efforts have to be redoubled, quadrupled, the warning clarions have to be sounded louder. Going over the cliff-edge would wake everyone up, but of course too late; so the education effort, and appeals even to the rawest self-interest, have to continue.

The effect sought from such efforts is for *people's primary instrument in this connection, their governments* to act with the global, not the national, interest in mind, in concert with other governments. In order to overcome the obstacle posed by politics and political careerism (politicians in government wish to stay in government, so their own careers count for them as a major concern and too often therefore as a barrier to interests that are not directly relevant to – and perhaps even contrary to – their career prospects), democracy has to be real and effective so that government is indeed, as it should be, the instrument of the people. This sentence captures the absolute key, the real solution, to the world's problems. To repeat: *genuine and effective democracy is the real key to solving the world's problems.*

Why, and how? The answer is: because the will of the people can break the self-interest Law as it applies to governments, international interest groups, and multinational corporations. It can stop what can be done from being done where its being done threatens harm; it can make happen what can be done and would be best to do but is being blocked by partisan interests. Note that in both formulations *what can be done* is at issue; stopping the negative *can be done* and enabling the positive *can be done* is what people can oblige their governments to do in circumstances of genuine and effective democracy.

And it only has to be achieved in the world's leading economies – the G7 states Canada, France, Germany, Italy, Japan, the UK, and the US, a couple of which are not far from being genuine democracies already (Germany and Japan), plus India and most of the other EU states; because these countries, and the pressure they are able jointly to apply to China and Russia, can do a very great deal together.[4]

An anecdotal aside illuminates the point about why democracy is the answer to the climate problem and the potential technological risks. (It is obvious why it is the answer to the justice deficit everywhere.) A number of years ago, on the basis of a UN report about the positive effects of education, even elementary education, on the lives of women in developing countries, I became interested in an initiative for a girls' school in Africa. I was advised by Ayaan Hirsi Ali that the school should be coeducational, not restricted just to girls, because the latter might suffer the resentment of the boys and men in their community. Instead, Ayaan said, the key to ensuring that girls benefit from education is to ensure that the school has a toilet with a door. This enables girls to continue with their education when puberty begins, because they can manage their personal hygiene at school instead of being unable to attend for as much as a cumulative quarter of the year, a factor that prompts many to drop out altogether. So: a key aspect to providing female education is not, or not just, books and blackboards and pencils and chalk, but something off to one side, as it were: *a toilet with a door*. In the past, when I lived in Africa, such schools as were available in rural districts of most sub-Saharan countries rarely possessed such a luxury. The school, if it existed, was likely to be a patch of ground under a tree, or a single room built of breeze-blocks with a corrugated iron roof – and nothing else.[5] The moral of this anecdote is that the key to a problem is sometimes not something we suppose is obvious and direct, but is off to one side, an unexpected element one might not see because one is not looking in that direction.

In like manner, the key to fully addressing the world's problems lies off to one side from climate conferences, debates about legislative controls on weapons systems and AI developments, and UN publications on human rights. It lies *in the ballot box*. But the ballot box has to do its job, in two crucial ways.

One is the degree of information possessed, and the thought applied, by the person putting a ballot into the ballot box, this person being one of an enfranchised portion of the population which is as extensive as possible, and all of whose members are required as a civic duty to vote.

The second is the effect of the votes thus cast, each vote counting equally with every other because all votes represent, in an authentically proportional manner, the spread of preferences of the voters.[6] In many of the world's democracies this condition is not met. For egregious examples, it is not met in the United States, the United Kingdom, Canada, or India, all of which use plurality ('first-past-the-post') voting systems that are intrinsically unrepresentative, frequently if not standardly resulting in the election of candidates and governments on minorities of votes cast, and squeezing out all but two political blocs with an interest in maintaining this system because it makes possible 100 per cent power on the support of just one-third of the electorate.[7]

Add to the inadequacy of the democracies in the US, India, Canada, and the UK the fact that democracy in Russia has some of the superficial forms but too little of the reality of democracy, and remember that China is a Party dictatorship.[8] Together these countries – chiefly the US, China, India, Russia – are the major players in causing the world's problems, and they therefore are the players whose actions need to change, because they are the ones which can make the needed difference. Those countries whose populations have a realistic chance of bringing their governments under full democratic control, therefore, acting together and jointly bringing pressure on China and Russia, are our hope; their people have to be properly and thoughtfully informed of the peril we all face – and then motivated to act on that information.

In essence, the information that needs to be disseminated as widely as possible is available and discussed in the foregoing pages.

The point to be borne in mind is that democracy – 'government by the people for the people' – is supposed to be a system in which people appoint a government to frame laws in their interest and administer those laws on their behalf. In its essence, accordingly, the theoretical idea of democracy is that government is *the servant of the people* – accountable to them, and removable by them if it does not do a satisfactory job. This theory has to be put into practice. It is not fully in practice in the US, India, Canada, and the UK. It is not in practice in Russia. It is nowhere near in practice in China, where effective opposition is always limited to the most extreme form: violent overthrow of dynasties, invasion (as by the Qing overthrowing the Ming in 1636) or mass rebellions short of dynasty change (like the 1850–64 Taiping Rebellion).

There are several fundamentals of democratic government. One is that by definition democratic government is for *all the people*, not just for a group, class, interest, or faction consisting only of some of the people – that is, not only those who voted for the political party that forms the government, and certainly not only those who funded that political party.

It follows from this, secondly, that democratic government is neither majoritarian nor minoritarian, but inclusive in its duties and aims. Society is made up of a diverse collection of individuals and minorities, and there is no such thing as 'a majority' except as a more or less temporary coalition of minorities formed around a particular issue. Democratic government is not majoritarian because not even a large majority can be allowed to overrule minority and individual rights. Democratic government is not minoritarian because a single faction cannot be allowed to dictate policies and laws and to administer them in its own exclusive interests. It has to be acknowledged that decision by majority agreement is often enough required; it is taken as a basis for action – unless it violates minority rights – when consensus cannot be reached, as often happens because of the diversity of views among minorities. But it is a compromise, though acceptable on rational grounds.

But despite the reliance on majority agreement when consensus is absent, the principle that the first duty of government is to serve the interests *of all* means that it has to transcend politics in this sense: that political differences of view about policy have to be subordinated to the public interest once the people have had their say *via* the ballot box. In a proportional electoral system the expression of voter preferences is unlikely to result in a legislature in which the representatives of just one party outnumber all the others combined. Decisions in the legislature will therefore require agreement among the parties present in it.

Compromise and agreement are the way that government rises above partisan political interests.

Party politics always has its place on the hustings and in the national debate, as it does in the negotiations that form a government – countries with proportional electoral systems sometimes take a long time to establish a government after an election; but this is often to the good, because it means that the eventual legislative programme is one more rather than less likely to capture what is important to different sections of the community, and to limit the degree to which any single partisan interest controls government action.

There are other desiderata of genuine democracy, such as constitutional clarity on the extent and limits of the powers given to those elected or employed to fill offices of state; the separation of powers between legislature, executive, and judiciary; the extent of the franchise and whether voting should be compulsory (I argue elsewhere that the voting age should be sixteen and voting should be a required civic duty); and more.[9] But a key component of ensuring genuine democracy is the voting system, which, whatever particular form it takes, should fully reflect the spread of interests and preferences among the enfranchised.

Proponents of the plurality 'first-past-the-post' (FPTP) system claim that it results in 'strong government' because it avoids coalitions based on back-room compromises and patchworks of policies. This overlooks the fact that every political party is internally a coalition where – even more hidden from public view – back-room deals and compromises are worked out, while yet having a constituency of supporters and backers whom they serve preferentially over the populace as a whole. But chiefly this defence of FPTP misses the essential point that it disenfranchises large numbers – indeed, often the *majority*

– of electors, and places government in the hands of just one of the competing political parties, in effect constituting an elective oligarchy.

To repeat: proportional representation tends to produce coalitions, and coalition governments, formed on a programme of compromises, are less likely to enact extreme versions of political ideologies. *Democratic* government is *for all*, so the tendency to politically moderate government has advantages, though doubtless frustrating to idealists of whatever cause. And in this situation too there is a further real virtue: the existence of policy opportunities for interests in society that are simply blanked out in the one-party government that follows an FPTP election.

Achieving a representative picture of preferences among the enfranchised is not the only desideratum. Another is that the electoral system should not result in very small parties holding government to ransom because they have the balance of power. The way to obviate this is by a minimum percentage vote to secure representation, and by constitutional requirements providing that certain central government responsibilities, such as security matters and the budget, cannot be delayed too long by a minority whose electoral support is below a certain percentage.

The argument that proportional representation allows extremist small parties into a legislature invites the following reply. If such a party secures a percentage of the vote, that indicates the presence of a group in society seeking representation, and in a democracy they have a right to be heard provided that they are not aiming to incite violence, discrimination, or hate. Secondly and more importantly, allowing such opinions to be expressed, discussed, and challenged in the legislature is a way of defusing their destabilizing potential, for if they are kept

outside the society's institutions they can profit from marginalization and can seem to have a larger importance than their actual
support warrants. If they are in the legislature on a proportional
representation system, their true size and significance is clear,
and they are consequently less of a threat. Moreover, it is undem-
ocratic to argue that, apart from incitements to violence,
discrimination, and hate, some views should not be allowed to
be aired in society, however unpalatable; freedom of expression
is not an unqualified good, but apart from specific circumstances
(keeping secrets in time of war, for example) it is fundamental
to the possession and exercise of all other rights and liberties,
and it cannot be limited by feelings of offence or societal
fashions.[10]

Some anti-democrats argue that it is a challengeable assumption of democracy that 'because the majority want X they must
have it', however unwise X might be from an objective standpoint. The response to this – 'Who says X is unwise? Who has
more authority on this matter than the majority?' – is regarded
as settling the matter on the self-same ground – that majority
will is enough. Leaving aside the point that majority will cannot
overrule minority rights, the anti-democrat might then ask: why
does the majority want X? Could they have been misinformed,
have they been led to believe a falsehood, are they acting on bad
impulses such as xenophobia or racism? This is in effect the
question: *should* they want X? Take, for example, the questions,
'Is it wise to smoke tobacco, binge-drink alcohol, drive too fast
along urban streets?' The point of the questions is to challenge
the idea that merely wanting X in large enough numbers
outweighs better-informed, more expert, or more considered
judgment about the value of X.

This illustrates a genuine dilemma, seeming to oppose a form
of paternalism to the idea that the ultimate holders of political

authority in a state are its people. But in fact the concept of *repre-sentative* democracy is precisely designed to resolve this dilemma, by honouring both the final authority of the people and the need for considered judgment on policy matters. Representative democracy is intended to serve the interests of all by sending people to find out and act upon information about what would best serve those interests – for example: setting up an education system, hospitals, medical staff, police for public security, and so on. Representatives are elected – in effect: employed – to do a job that requires information and judgment, just as with doctors, airline pilots, and teachers. This requires that electors be careful to send *good* representatives to the legis-lature, not just accepting whoever the local political party of their preference puts forward.

These remarks outline what is meant by *genuine democracy*.[11] It was mentioned in the Introduction that the third arena of the world's problems – justice and rights – underlies the other two, in the sense that their *absence* is a reason for the invariable opera-tions of the self-interest Law. If you are without a vote, if you live in an environment where information is not freely available, if campaigning to change or oppose government behaviour is met with repression, you are of course very far from any kind of democracy, and can do little towards what is required. It is diffi-cult enough to inform people in a democracy and to get them to use their power as voters to make a difference; it is difficult enough to reform electoral systems that are unrepresentative and simply result in power being passed around from one politi-cal clique to another. How much harder, therefore, is it for the hundreds of millions of people who do not have genuine or even any democracy, who live under the many kinds of constraint that deny them a voice or influence, to make a contribution?

It is implicit in the discussion of justice and rights, and in the observation that many hundreds of millions of people have at best incomplete access to them, that the common set of values that would be operative in – because they are the principal values of – genuine democracy, is the set captured in the discourse of human rights. Note therefore the line of reasoning at work here: genuine democracy is the means to get selfless cooperation among governments; genuine democracy is the embodiment and enactment of human rights; the answer to the question: *Can there be a system of universal values that all could share, enabling global cooperation to deal with global threats?* is therefore: *Yes; it is the framework of human rights.*

As they are stated in summary form in declarations and schedules – the right to life, to privacy, to due process at law, and so on – the principles of human rights are clear enough. They merit examination and discussion in detail, because they are rich in implications. Take, for example, the 'right to life'. This cannot be a right to bare existence merely; it implies a minimum quality of life, a life worth living for the person living it. You are not honouring a person's right to life by locking him in a tiny cage and feeding him bread and water occasionally, enough to keep him alive. What therefore is the minimum quality of life? Consider the following situation: suppose a person's quality of life has dropped irrecoverably below a limit acceptable to herself because of illness or disability; suppose that she therefore desires to bring her life to an end because her suffering is unendurable; and suppose that she is physically incapable of committing suicide. Does her right to life – life of a certain minimum quality – entail a correlative right to have her request for an easeful death honoured? It is obvious what supporters and opponents of a 'right to die' would contrastingly say in response; but the question shows how the rights listed in the Universal

Declaration, the European Convention on Human Rights, and other such instruments, both outline and invite discussion about fundamental values.[12]

Another example is access to law, its protection, and its remedies. The expense – particularly the expense – and delay that attend legal proceedings are serious practical barriers to access to law for most people; and that means that a fundamental human right is denied them. Articles 6–11 of the Universal Declaration (thus six out of the twenty-seven articles which are specifically about rights as such) concern the rights to recognition as a person before the law, equal protection of the law, effective remedy at law, the law's protection against arbitrary arrest and detention, a fair hearing before a court, and the right to be regarded as innocent until proved guilty. Justice delayed, it is rightly said, is justice denied. But the enormous cost of litigation, exacerbated by the fact that the best lawyers cost the most to hire, introduces the distorting effect of money into Article 10's 'full equality to a fair and public hearing'.

It is only a minority of the world's population that has the luxury even of an expensive and slow legal system, which shows how far in general the world is from the benefits that full possession and exercise of human rights would confer. In a genuine democracy, access to law would not merely be a right but an exercisable right. The same would apply to the other rights agreed as fundamental to the chance for good individual lives in a good society – and as constituting the framework of the kind of democracy in question.

Genuine democracy in the major economies of the world where it is feasibly attainable, and everywhere promoting the justice and rights embodied in human rights instruments, is accordingly the best hope we have of the world joining hands to confront its challenges. In the leading economies, getting the right kind of voter (informed, thoughtful, altruistic) and the right kind of system (inclusive, proportional) seems as utopian as the ideal of getting the world's governments to act selflessly together. But to repeat: it is our best hope.

Is it the only hope? Not quite. There is another way that the harmful *can be done* can be stopped and the positive *can be done* can be achieved – a rather less desirable way, admittedly, than the foregoing, but still better than catastrophe. This is activisms *imposing* the costs that governments and corporations are unwilling to bear, thus making them stop what good can be done, or continuing to do harmful things because they can be done and 'everyone else is probably doing them'. Widespread disruptive activism of the Extinction Rebellion kind would be an example of imposing such costs. My guess is that if voters and their governments do not take the considered course, such activism – as catastrophe comes closer, and panic grows – will increasingly be the recourse adopted. The choices therefore are between people and their governments accepting the cost, or some people imposing the cost – or having reality impose a vastly greater and perhaps fatal cost.

At the moment in which these words are written, the last of these alternatives is the most likely one.

BIBLIOGRAPHY

James Barratt, *Our Final Invention* (New York: St Martin's Press, 2013)

Jeremy Bentham, 'Anarchical Fallacies', in John Bowring (ed.), *The Works of Jeremy Bentham*, Vol. 2 (Edinburgh: William Tate, 1838–43)

Ariane Bigenwald and Valerian Chambon, 'Criminal Responsibility and Neuroscience: No Revolution Yet', *Frontiers in Psychology*, 10 (2019), www.frontiersin.org/articles/10.3389/fpsyg.2019.01406/full

Nick Bostrom, *Superintelligence: Paths, Dangers, Strategies* (Oxford: Oxford University Press, 2014)

Nick Bostrom and Eliezer Yudkowsky, 'The Ethics of Artificial Intelligence', in *The Cambridge Companion to Artificial Intelligence* (Cambridge: Cambridge University Press, 2014)

Nigel M. de S. Cameron, *Will Robots Take Your Job?* (Malden: Polity Press, 2017)

R. A. Clarke, *Cyber War* (London: HarperCollins, 2010)

Climate Crisis Advisory Group, 'The Global Climate Crisis and the Action Needed', 21 June 2021, https://static1.squarespace.com/static/60ccae65 8553d102459d11ed/t/60d421c67f1dc67d682d8d29/1624515027604 /CCAG+Launch+Paper.pdf

Antonio Damasio, *Descartes' Error* (New York: G.P. Putnam, 1994)

Kate Devlin, *Turned On: Science, Sex and Robots* (London: Bloomsbury, 2020)

Ben Ehrenreich, 'We're Hurtling towards Global Suicide', *New Republic*, 18 March 2021

Elizabeth Evans, *The Politics of Third Wave Feminisms: Neoliberalism, Intersectionality, and the State in Britain and the US* (London: Palgrave Macmillan, 2015)

M. Fabiani et al., 'True but Not False Memories Produce a Sensory Signature in Human Lateralised Brain Potentials', *Journal of Cognitive Neuroscience*, 12 (2000)

L. A. Farwell and S. S. Smith, 'Using Brain MERMER Testing to Detect Knowledge Despite Efforts to Conceal', *Journal of Forensic Science*, 46 (2001)

Eduard Fosch-Villaronga and Adam Poulsen, 'Sex Care Robots', *Paladyn, Journal of Behavioral Robotics*, 11 (2020), www.degruyter.com/document /doi/10.1515/pjbr-2020-0001/html

Robert Garland, *The Greek Way of Life* (Ithaca: Cornell University Press, 1990)

Bill Gates, *How to Avoid a Climate Disaster* (London: Allen Lane, 2021)

Jonathan Glover, *What Sort of People Should There Be?* (London: Pelican, 1984)

I. J. Good, 'Speculations Concerning the First Ultra Intelligent Machine', in F. L. Alt and M. Rubinoff (eds), *Advances in Computers*, Vol. 6 (New York: Academic Press, 1965)

A. C. Grayling, *Democracy and Its Crisis* (London: Oneworld, 2017)

— *Descartes: The Life and Times of a Genius* (London: Free Press, 2005)

— *Ideas That Matter* (London: Weidenfeld & Nicolson, 2009)

— *Refutation of Scepticism* (Aurora, IL: Open Court, 1985)

— *The Age of Genius* (London: Bloomsbury, 2017)

— *The Frontiers of Knowledge* (London: Viking Penguin, 2021)

— *The Good State* (London: Oneworld, 2020)

— *The History of Philosophy* (London: Viking, 2019)

— *Towards the Light* (London: Bloomsbury, 2007)

— *War* (London: Yale University Press, 2017)

P. Haggard and M. Eimer, 'On the Relation Between Brain Potentials and the Awareness of Voluntary Movements', *Experimental Brain Research*, 126 (1999)

J. D. Hamblin, *Oceanographers and the Cold War* (Seattle: University of Washington Press, 2005)

IPCC (Intergovernmental Panel on Climate Change) 'Summary for Policymakers', in *Climate Change 2013: The Physical Science Basis. Contribution of Working Group I to the Fifth Assessment Report of the Intergovernmental Panel on Climate Change*, ed. T. F. Stocker, D. Qin, G.-K. Plattner, M. Tignor, S. K. Allen, J. Boschung, A. Nauels, Y. Xia, V. Bex and P. M. Midgley (Cambridge and New York: Cambridge University Press, 2013)

Daniel Kahneman, *Thinking, Fast and Slow* (London: Penguin, 2013)

J. Kelly, 'Is Football Bigotry Confined to the West of Scotland? The Heart of Midlothian and Hibernian Rivalry', in J. Flint and J. Kelly (eds), *Bigotry*,

Football and Scotland (Edinburgh: Edinburgh University Press, 2013), www.pure.ed.ac.uk/ws/portalfiles/portal/15242619/Is_football_bigotry_confined_to_the_west_of_Scotland.pdf

David Levy, *Love and Sex with Robots* (London: Duckworth, 2009)

B. Libet, 'Unconscious Cerebral Initiative and the Role of Conscious Will in Voluntary Action', *Behavioral Brain Science*, 8 (1985)

John Locke, *Second Treatise of Government* (1689)

J. L. Mackie, *Ethics* (London: Penguin, 1977)

Michael E. Mann, *The New Climate War* (London: Scribe UK, 2021)

Alexander Nauels et al., 'Linking Sea Level Rise and Socioeconomic Indicators under the Shared Socioeconomic Pathways', *Environmental Research Letters*, 12 (2017), 114002

Jacquetta A. Newman and Linda Ann White, *Women, Politics, and Public Policy*, 2nd ed. (Toronto: Oxford University Press, 2012)

Robert Nozick, *Anarchy, State, and Utopia* (New York: Basic Books, 1974)

Helen Pankhurst, *Deeds Not Words* (London: Sceptre, 2018)

Derek Parfitt, *Reasons and Persons* (Oxford: Oxford University Press, 1987)

Nick Polson and James Scott, *AIQ: How Artificial Intelligence Works and How We Can Harness Its Power for a Better World* (London: Transworld, 2018)

Richard Posner, *Sex and Reason* (Cambridge, MA: Harvard University Press, 1992)

A. Raine, J. R. Meloy, S. Bihrle et al., 'Reduced Prefrontal and Increased Sub-Cortical Brain Functioning Assessed Using Positron Emission Tomography in Predatory and Affective Murderers', *Behavioral Sciences and the Law*, 16 (1998)

John Rawls, *A Theory of Justice* (Cambridge, MA: Belknap Press, rev. ed., 1999)

Antonio Regalado, 'Elon Musk's Neuralink Is Neuroscience Theater', *MIT Technology Review*, 30 August 2020, www.technologyreview.com/2020/08/30/1007786/elon-musks-neuralink-demo-update-neuroscience-theater/

M. A. Roberts, 'The Nonidentity Problem', *The Stanford Encyclopedia of Philosophy* (2019), plato.stanford.edu/entries/nonidentity-problem/

William Robinson, 'Philosophical Challenges', in Keith Frankish and William M. Ramsay (eds), *The Cambridge Companion to Artificial Intelligence* (Cambridge: Cambridge University Press, 2014)

Sarah W. Rodriguez, 'Rethinking the History of Female Circumcision and Clitoridectomy', *Journal of the History of Medicine and Allied Sciences*, 63 (2008)

Kristin Rowe-Finkbeiner, *The F Word: Feminism in Jeopardy* (Emeryville, CA: Seal Press, 2004)

William Shakespeare, *King Lear* (1606–8)

Noel Sharkey, Aimee van Wynsberghe, Scott Robbins, and Eleanor Hancock, *Our Sexual Future with Robots* (The Hague: Foundation for Responsible Robotics, 2017. Pdf. Archived 8 July 2017 at the Wayback Machine)

S. C. Sherwood and M. Huber, 'An Adaptability Limit to Climate Change Due to Heat Stress', *Proceedings of the National Academy of Sciences*, 107, 21 (2010)

Peter Singer, *The Most Good You Can Do* (New Haven: Yale University Press, 2015)

Susan B. Sorenson, 'Gender Disparities in Injury Mortality: Consistent, Persistent, and Larger Than You'd Think', *American Journal of Public Health*, 101 (2011), www.ncbi.nlm.nih.gov/pmc/articles/PMC3222499

John Studd, 'Ovariotomy for Menstrual Madness and Premenstrual Syndrome – 19th Century History and Lessons for Current Practice', *Gynecological Endocrinology*, 22 (2006), www.tandfonline.com/doi/full/10.1080/09513590600881503

— 'A Comparison of 19th Century and Contemporary Attitudes to Female Sexuality', *Gynecological Endocrinology*, 23 (2007), https://pubmed.ncbi.nlm.nih.gov/18075842

John P. Sullins, 'Robots, Love, and Sex: The Ethics of Building a Love Machine', *IEEE Transactions on Affective Computing*, 3, 4 (January 2012)

Richard Susskind and Daniel Susskind, *The Future of the Professions* (Oxford: Oxford University Press, 2015)

Cecilia Tasca, Mariangela Rapetti, Mauro Giovanni Carta, and Bianca Fadda, 'Women and Hysteria in the History of Mental Health', *Clinical Practice & Epidemiology in Mental Health*, 8 (2012)

Max Tegmark, *Life 3.0: Being Human in the Age of Artificial Intelligence* (New York: Knopf, 2017)

Barbara Tuchman, *The Proud Tower* (London: Penguin, 2014 ed.)

Stefano Vassanelli, 'Brain-Chip Interfaces: the Present and the Future', *Procedia Computer Sciences*, 7 (2011), www.sciencedirect.com/science/article/pii/S1877050911006855

Mary Wollstonecraft, *A Vindication of the Rights of Woman* (London: Penguin Classics, rev. ed., 2004)

NOTES

1 Confronting the Danger of a Warming World

1 While this book was in proof the EU announced an intention to cut CO_2e emissions by 55% by 2030. This is the most positive advance to date.

2 Fossil fuels are hydrocarbons. Not all hydrocarbons are derived from biological remains.

3 J. D. Hamblin, *Oceanographers and the Cold War* (Seattle: University of Washington Press, 2005).

4 'Atmospheric CO2 Passes 420 ppm for First Time Ever', *EcoWatch*, 7 April 2021, www.ecowatch.com/carbon-dioxide-exceeds-420-2651380906.html (retrieved 17 April 2021).

5 UN Convention to Combat Desertification, 'Sustainability, Stability, Security', www.unccd.int/sustainability-stability-security (retrieved 16 March 2021).

6 See WWF, 'Half of Plant and Animal Species at Risk from Climate Change in World's Most Important Natural Places', 14 March 2018, www.worldwildlife.org/press-releases/half-of-plant-and-animal-species -at-risk-from-climate-change-in-world-s-most-important-natural-places (retrieved 18 March 2021), and Royal Gardens Kew, *State of the World's Plants and Fungi 2020*, www.kew.org/science/state-of-the-worlds-plants -and-fungi (retrieved 16 March 2021).

7 'Hazards and Risks of Climate Change Impacts', *EU Science Hub*, https:/ /ec.europa.eu/jrc/en/research-topic/hazards-and-risks-climate-change -impacts (retrieved 16 March 2021).

8 IPCC (Intergovernmental Panel on Climate Change) 'Summary for Policy-makers', in *Climate Change 2013: The Physical Science Basis. Contribution of Working Group I to the Fifth Assessment Report of the Intergovernmental Panel on Climate Change*, ed. T. F. Stocker, D. Qin, G.-K. Plattner, M. Tignor, S. K. Allen, J. Boschung, A. Nauels, Y. Xia, V. Bex and P. M. Midgley (Cambridge and New York: Cambridge University Press, 2013). See also updates in IPCC Sixth Assessment Report, 2021.

9 UNFCCC, 'The Paris Agreement', https://unfccc.int/process-and-meetings/the-paris-agreement/the-paris-agreement (retrieved 16 March 2021).

10 Alistair Walsh, 'John Kerry calls on EU to reduce emissions within 10 years', *DW.com*, 18 May 2021, www.dw.com/en/john-kerry-calls-on-eu-to-reduce-emissions-within-10-years/a-57574661 (retrieved 22 June 2021).

11 Alexander Nauels, 'Linking Sea Level Rise and Socioeconomic Indicators under the Shared Socioeconomic Pathways', *Environmental Research Letters*, 12 (2017), 114002.

12 Richard Ernst, 'Venus Was Once More Earth-Like, But Climate Change Made It Uninhabitable', *EarthSky*, 20 December 2020, https://earthsky.org/space/venus-was-once-earthlike-climate-change (retrieved 16 March 2021).

13 S. C. Sherwood and M. Huber, 'An Adaptability Limit to Climate Change Due to Heat Stress', *Proceedings of the National Academy of Sciences* 107, No. 21 (2010), 9552–5.

14 Michael E. Mann, *The New Climate War* (London: Scribe UK, 2021). I am indebted to his excellent account here.

15 Ibid., p. 3.

16 As one example: there were 2,210 crude oil tankers registered globally in 2020, over 800 of them very large; 'Number of Crude Oil Tankers Worldwide as of April 2020 by Type', *Statista*, www.statista.com/statistics/468405/global-oil-tanker-fleet-by-type (retrieved 17 March 2021).

17 Mann, *The New Climate War*, p. 2.

18 Ibid., p. 5.

19 Alejandra Borunda, 'The Most Consequential Impact of Trump's Climate Policies? Wasted Time,' *National Geographic*, 11 December 2020, www.nationalgeographic.com/environment/article/most-consequential-impact-of-trumps-climate-policies-wasted-time (retrieved 17 March 2021).

20 Mann, *The New Climate War*, p. 6.

21 Ibid.

22 Ibid.

23 Bill Gates, 'Here's How the US Can Lead the World on Climate Change Innovation', *GatesNotes*, 3 December 2020, www.gatesnotes.com/ Energy/How-the-US-can-lead-on-climate-change-innovation (retrieved 28 April 2021).

24 Mann, *The New Climate War*, p. 200.

25 Ibid., p. 202.

26 Ibid., p. 204.

27 Ibid., pp. 204–5.

28 Ibid., pp. 205–8.

29 Ibid., p. 216.

30 Ben Ehrenreich, 'We're Hurtling towards Global Suicide', *New Republic*, 18 March 2021.

31 Ibid.

32 Ibid.

33 Bill Gates, *How to Avoid a Climate Disaster* (London: Allen Lane, 2021), p. 195.

34 Ehrenreich, 'We're Hurtling towards Global Suicide'.

35 IEA World Energy Outlook 2020, www.iea.org/reports/world-energy-outlook-2020 (retrieved 16 June 2020).

36 Hannah Ritchie and Max Roser, 'Renewable Energy', *Our World in Data*, https://ourworldindata.org/renewable-energy (retrieved 21 March 2021).

37 Gates has a number of suggestions on these same lines, persuasively put; see his *How to Avoid a Climate Disaster*, chapter 12, 'What Each of Us Can Do', pp. 217 et seq.

38 This theory is defended by J. L. Mackie in his classic *Ethics* (London: Penguin, 1977).

39 A personal note on this theme is appropriate here. While attending the UN Commission on Human Rights in Geneva in the 1990s I read a UN report on the positive effect of even just a few years' elementary education on the quality of life of African women. I became enthusiastic about supporting girls' education on that continent, given my own associations with it; and was counselled by Ayaan Hirsi Ali that the secret to girls' ability to continue with education after the onset of puberty was provision of toilet facilities at schools. This kind of sidebar consideration too often escapes thinking about how to make initiatives effective.

40 Tom Bawden, 'Women Are More Vulnerable to Dangers of Global Warming Than Men', *Independent*, 2 November 2015, p. 11.

41 Much more technical versions of this argument are debated by philosophers working in climate ethics; among the distinguished contributors

to the debate was Derek Parfitt; see his *Reasons and Persons* (Oxford: Oxford University Press, 1987). For an excellent introduction to the issues and a full bibliography, see M. A. Roberts, 'The Nonidentity Problem', *The Stanford Encyclopedia of Philosophy* (2019), https://plato. stanford.edu/entries/nonidentity-problem/ (retrieved 22 March 2021).

42 The precarious nature of the world's response to climate change is illustrated with increasing frequency in mainstream news; a speaking example is afforded by the *Washington Post* announcing on 5 April 2021 that atmospheric CO_2 concentrations had reached 420 ppm, halfway to doubling the level in the pre-industrial atmosphere; Matthew Cappucci and Jason Samenow, 'Carbon dioxide spikes to critical record, halfway to doubling preindustrial levels', *Washington Post*, 5 April 2021, https:// apple.news/ADE2ETIfAQEq5XaNyhJ8cxQ (retrieved 18 June 2021). The next day Britain's *iNews* reported that on the preceding Monday, an Easter bank holiday with mild sunny weather, zero-carbon sources had provided 80 per cent of the nation's energy, the 'greenest-ever day' recorded: wind provided 29 per cent, solar 21 per cent, nuclear 16 per cent, with gas providing only 10 per cent, the remainder coming from biomass and imports, no coal being burned that day. In fact coal-powered generation had dropped dramatically in any case, providing only 1.6 per cent of the UK's energy in 2020, down from 25 per cent in 2015. Greenpeace UK welcomed the figures, but warned that emissions from the transport, agriculture and domestic sectors were still too high and needed more vigorous regulation. Nick Duffy, 'Britain's Electricity Grid Had "Greenest Ever" Day on Easter Monday', *iNews*, 6 April 2021, https: //inews.co.uk/news/environment/britains-electricity-grid-greenest-ever-day-easter-monday-945359 (retrieved 18 June 2021).

43 Climate Crisis Advisory Group, 'The Global Climate Crisis and the Action Needed,' 21 June 2021, https://static1.squarespace.com/static/60ccae6585 53d102459d11ed/t/60d421c67f1dc67d682d8d29/1624515027604/ CCAG+Launch+Paper.pdf (retrieved 6 October 2021).

2 Technology and the Future

1 A survey of the history of technology from Palaeolithic times to the dawn of modern science is given in A. C. Grayling, *The Frontiers of Knowledge* (London: Viking Penguin, 2021).

2 More on this later, but I argue as much in *Democracy and Its Crisis* (London: Oneworld, 2017) and *The Good State* (London: Oneworld, 2020).

3 See Nigel M. de S. Cameron, *Will Robots Take Your Job?* (Malden: Polity Press, 2017).
4 Ibid., pp. 15–17.
5 Richard Susskind and Daniel Susskind, *The Future of the Professions* (Oxford: Oxford University Press, 2015), ebook loc. 7690.
6 Bryan Lufkin, 'What the world can learn from Japan's robots', *BBC Worklife*, 6 February 2020, www.bbc.com/worklife/article/20200205-what-the-world-can-learn-from-japans-robots (retrieved 24 March 2021).
7 Pararobots, www.parorobots.com (retrieved 24 March 2021).
8 See Realbotix, https://realbotix.com (retrieved 24 March 2021).
9 John P. Sullins, 'Robots, Love, and Sex: The Ethics of Building a Love Machine', *IEEE Transactions on Affective Computing* 3, 4 (January 2012), 398–409.
10 Noel Sharkey, Aimee van Wynsberghe, Scott Robbins, and Eleanor Hancock, *Our Sexual Future with Robots* (The Hague: Foundation for Responsible Robotics, 2017. Pdf. Archived 8 July 2017 at the Wayback Machine).
11 See Campaign Against Sex Robots, https://campaignagainstsexrobots.org (retrieved 24 March 2021).
12 Eduard Fosch-Villaronga and Adam Poulsen, 'Sex Care Robots', *Paladyn, Journal of Behavioral Robotics*, 11 (2020), www.degruyter.com/document/doi/10.1515/pjbr-2020-0001/html (retrieved 24 March 2021).
13 'Spurious Logic Used to Justify Child Sex Dolls', *ABC*, www.abc.net.au/religion/spurious-logic-used-to-justify-child-sex-dolls/11856284 (retrieved 24 March 2021).
14 A side-speculation about the difference between the attitudes of men and women to sex robots, together with the evidence from more promiscuous forms of male homosexual practice such as 'cottaging', prompts a reminder: that most human experience of intimacy, caring, companionship, affection, and bonding is independent of sexual behaviour. In many cultures, and in the history of Western culture itself, the idea that sexual expression must always and only, or at very least standardly, be contextualized in such bonding, has not been the norm. The suppression of opportunities for sexual expression, one major form of this being the expectation that it is to be wholly or mainly contained in the context of this kind of relationship, has been argued to be harmful, with a spectrum of problems being laid at its door from aberrant behaviour to divorce. As Richard Posner points out in *Sex and Reason* (Cambridge, MA: Harvard University Press, 1992), monogamy and prostitution are symbiotic, a fact that is a speaking comment on the romantic desire to constrain sexuality within socially conservative structures.

15 See David Levy, *Love and Sex With Robots* (London: Duckworth, 2009); Kate Devlin, *Turned On: Science, Sex and Robots* (London: Bloomsbury, 2020).

16 See Dan Keating, Kevin Schaul, and Leslie Shapiro, 'The Facebook Ads Russians Targeted at Different Groups', *Washington Post*, 1 November 2017, www.washingtonpost.com/graphics/2017/business/russian-ads-facebook-targeting/ (retrieved 18 June 2021). For 2020 a useful overview is given in 'Russian Interference in the 2020 United States Elections', *Wikipedia*, https://en.wikipedia.org/wiki/Russian_interference_in_the_2020_United_States_elections (retrieved 24 March 2021).

17 Stefano Vassanelli, 'Brain-Chip Interfaces: the Present and the Future', *Procedia Computer Sciences*, 7 (2011), 61–4, www.sciencedirect.com/science/article/pii/S1877050911006855 (retrieved 24 March 2021).

18 At the outset of discussion of AI one encounters the question of how to define intelligence, what different kinds of intelligence there are, whether intelligence can only be predicated of biological entities, and more; I leave these complexities aside here apart from the explicit and implicit characterizations given in the discussion that follows. For a more detailed look at some of the issues, see William Robinson, 'Philosophical Challenges', in Keith Frankish and William M. Ramsay (eds), *The Cambridge Companion to Artificial Intelligence* (Cambridge: Cambridge University Press, 2014), pp. 64–85.

19 James Barratt, *Our Final Invention* (London: St Martin's Press, 2013), p. 3.

20 Ibid., pp. 4–5.

21 The classic argument to this effect is given by Leibniz. See A. C. Grayling, *The History of Philosophy* (London: Viking, 2019), p. 236.

22 As a later point makes clear, this depends on what the interests of all concerned are, and what relative weightings they merit. Consider, for example, the question, 'Is the survival of the orchid and the elephant more important than the potential for further human productions in the manner of Plato, Shakespeare, and Beethoven?' A case can be made for 'Yes' and a case can be made for 'No'. Determining which is the more persuasive goes to the heart of the issue here.

23 Barratt, *Our Final Invention*, p. 4.

24 Nick Bostrom, *Superintelligence: Paths, Dangers, Strategies* (Oxford: Oxford University Press, 2014), p. v. See also Max Tegmark, *Life 3.0: Being Human in the Age of Artificial Intelligence* (New York: Knopf, 2017).

25 Bostrom, *Superintelligence*.

26 I. J. Good, 'Speculations Concerning the First Ultraintelligent Machine',

in F. L. Alt and M. Rubinoff (eds), *Advances in Computers*, Vol. 6 (New York: Academic Press, 1965), pp. 31–88.

27 'AI' and 'machine learning' (ML) are not coterminous concepts. For a long period after the 1950s the two fields were regarded as distinct; some still regard them so, while others cite ML as a subset of AI.

28 Nick Polson and James Scott, *AIQ: How Artificial Intelligence Works and How We Can Harness Its Power for a Better World* (London: Transworld, 2018), p. 9.

29 Nick Bostrom and Eliezer Yudkowsky, 'The Ethics of Artificial Intelligence', in *The Cambridge Companion to Artificial Intelligence* (Cambridge: Cambridge University Press, 2014), pp. 316–23.

30 Ibid., p. 317.

31 See ProPublica's audit of sentencing bias: Julia Angwin, Jeff Larson, Surya Mattu, and Lauren Kirchner, 'Machine Bias', ProPublica, 23 May 2016, www.propublica.org/article/machine-bias-risk-assessments-in-criminal-sentencing (retrieved 18 June 2021).

32 Ibid., p. 316.

33 Ibid., p. 317.

34 Ibid., pp. 317–18.

35 'Research Priorities for Robust and Beneficial Artificial Intelligence', Future of Life Institute, https://futureoflife.org/ai-open-letter (retrieved 27 March 2021).

36 Stuart Russell, Daniel Dewey, and Max Tegmark, 'Research Priorities for Robust and Beneficial Artificial Intelligence', Association for the Advancement of Artificial Intelligence (2015), https://futureoflife.org/data/documents/research_priorities.pdf?x72900 (retrieved 27 March 2021).

37 A presentation on this issue was made by Jeff Hancock to the New College of the Humanities/Northeastern University Information Ethics Roundtable in April 2021.

38 Reality Defender 2020, https://rd2020.org (retrieved 27 March 2021).

39 For a survey of the incidents, see '2010 Flash Crash', *Wikipedia*, https://en.wikipedia.org/wiki/2010_flash_crash (retrieved 6 April 2021).

40 See A. C. Grayling, *War* (London: Yale University Press, 2017), pp. 165–7. I draw on my discussion there for this section of the discussion here.

41 I say 'he' and 'his,' but increasingly male exclusivity in combat roles is on the way out as these words are written.

42 The dumdum bullet – named after the British military cantonment of Dum Dum outside Calcutta – was developed by the British because the wounding effect of standard bullets on, for example, Afghani and Zulu tribesmen was insufficient to stop them fighting. Barbara Tuchman in

The Proud Tower (London: Penguin, 2014 ed.) quoted a British officer representing the British Army's case at the Hague Convention of 1899 on the question of hollow-point bullets as follows: 'Men penetrated through and through several times by our latest pattern of small calibre projectiles, which make small clean holes, are nevertheless able to rush on and come to close quarters. Some means had to be found to stop them. The civilized soldier when shot recognizes that he is wounded and knows that the sooner he is attended to the sooner he will recover. He lies down on his stretcher and is taken off the field to his ambulance, where he is dressed or bandaged. Your fanatical barbarian, similarly wounded, continues to rush on, spear or sword in hand; and before you have the time to represent to him that his conduct is in flagrant violation of the understanding relative to the proper course for the wounded man to follow – he may have cut off your head' (p. 293).

43 US Department of the Navy, 'The Navy Unmanned Undersea Vehicle (UUV) Master Plan', quoted in Grayling, *War*, p. 230.

44 Campaign to Stop Killer Robots, www.stopkillerrobots.org (retrieved 27 March 2021).

45 Antonio Damasio, *Descartes' Error* (New York: G.P. Putnam, 1994).

46 Nicola Davis, 'Scientists create online games to show risks of AI emotion recognition', *Guardian*, 4 April 2021, www.theguardian.com/technology/2021/apr/04/online-games-ai-emotion-recognition-emojify (retrieved 5 April 2021).

47 Human Rights Watch, 'Losing Humanity: The Case Against Killer Robots', 19 November 2012, www.hrw.org/report/2012/11/19/losing-humanity/case-against-killer-robots (retrieved 16 June 2021).

48 Ibid.

49 R. A. Clarke, *Cyber War* (New York: Ecco, 2010).

50 Reported in the *New York Times*, 14 April 2010.

51 This matter is discussed at more length in Grayling, *War*.

52 Nick Bostrom, 'What Happens When Our Computers Get Smarter Than We Are?', TED Talk, www.ted.com/talks/nick_bostrom_what_happens_when_our_computers_get_smarter_than_we_are; Sam Harris, 'How Can we Build AI without Losing Control Over It?', TED Talk, www.ted.com/talks/sam_harris_can_we_build_ai_without_losing_control_over_it (retrieved 18 June 2021).

53 Vassanelli, 'Brain-Chip Interfaces'. In this section I make use of discussion from the section on neuroscientific research in my *Frontiers of Knowledge* (London: Viking, 2021).

54 M. Fabiani et al., 'True but not False Memories Produce a Sensory

Signature in Human Lateralised Brain Potentials', *Journal of Cognitive Neuroscience*, 12 (2000), pp. 941–9. See also Farwell and Smith on the P -300 MERMER test which measures a wave potential obtained by exposing a subject to a stimulus which appears if associated with a genuine memory. Experiments suggest that the technique has an error ratio of less than 1 per cent. L. A. Farwell and S. S. Smith, 'Using Brain MERMER Testing to Detect Knowledge Despite Efforts to Conceal', *Journal of Forensic Science*, 46 (2001), 135–43.

55 For one example: Anil Seth says in his Royal Institution lecture, cited, that researchers at Glasgow University have made advances in this respect; Anil Seth, 'The Neuroscience of Consciousness', www.youtube. com/watch?v=xRel1JKOEbI, at 28 minutes 30 seconds, quoting L. Muckli et al., 'Contextual Feedback to Superficial Layers of V1', *Current Biology*, 25 (2015), pp. 2690–95.

56 A. Raine, J. R. Meloy, S. Bihrle, et al., 'Reduced Prefrontal and Increased Sub-Cortical Brain Functioning Assessed Using Positron Emission Tomography in Predatory and Affective Murderers', *Behavioral Sciences and the Law*, 16 (1998), pp. 319–32.

57 Ariane Bigenwald and Valerian Chambon, 'Criminal Responsibility and Neuroscience: No Revolution Yet', *Frontiers in Psychology*, 10 (2019), www.frontiersin.org/articles/10.3389/fpsyg.2019.01406/full (retrieved 6 April 2021).

58 B. Libet, 'Unconscious Cerebral Initiative and the Role of Conscious Will in Voluntary Action', *Behavioral Brain Science*, 8 (1985), 529–66; P. Haggard and M. Eimer, 'On the Relation between Brain Potentials and the Awareness of Voluntary Movements', *Experimental Brain Research*, 126 (1999), 128–33.

59 Duke University, 'Policy on Academic Dishonesty', 2014, http://studentaffairs.duke.edu/conduct/z-policies/academic-dishonesty (retrieved 6 April 2021).

60 DARPA, 'DARPA and the Brain Initiative', www.darpa.mil/program/our-research/darpa-and-the-brain-initiative (retrieved 6 April 2021).

61 See the discussion of this in Grayling, *War*, pp. 170–84.

62 Denver Nicks, 'Report: Suicide Rate Soars Among Young Vets', *Time*, 10 January 2014, https://time.com/304/report-suicide-rate-soars-among-young-vets/ (retrieved 23 May 2014): 'The suicide rate among veterans remains well above that for the general population, with roughly 20 former servicemen and women committing suicide every day.'

63 Adam Gabbatt, 'China Conducting Biological Tests to Create Super

Soldiers, US Spy Chief Says', *Guardian*, 4 December 2020, www.theguardian.com/world/2020/dec/04/china-super-soldiers-biologically-enhanced-john-ratcliffe (retrieved 6 April 2021).

64 'Elon Musk Unveils Pigs Implanted with Neuralink Brain Chip', YouTube, 29 August 2020, www.youtube.com/watch?v=kdCOHbx-gto (retrieved 6 April 2021); 'Elon Musk Startup Shows Monkey with Brain Chip Implants Playing Video Game', *Guardian*, 9 April 2021, www.theguardian.com/technology/2021/apr/09/elon-musk-neuralink-monkey-video-game (retrieved 10 April 2021).

65 Antonio Regalado, 'Elon Musk's Neuralink Is Neuroscience Theater', *MIT Technology Review*, 30 August 2020, www.technologyreview.com/2020/08/30/1007786/elon-musks-neuralink-demo-update-neuroscience-theater/ (retrieved 3 September 2020).

66 Amanda Heidt, 'New Report Dissects Ethics of Emerging Human Brain Cell Models', *Scientist*, 12 April 2021, www.the-scientist.com/news-opinion/new-report-dissects-ethics-of-emerging-human-brain-cell-models-68661 (retrieved 13 April 2021).

67 *Cell*, www.cell.com (retrieved 16 April 2021).

68 Sam Hancock, 'Scientists "Open Pandora's Box" with Human-Monkey Chimeric Embryo', *Independent*, 16 April 2021, www.independent.co.uk/independentpremium/human-monkey-embryo-chimeras-research-b1832337.html (retrieved 16 April 2021). As evidence of the ethical concerns felt about the creation of chimaeras, which researchers argue provides hope for creation of organs suitable for transplant into human patients, the *Independent* described the research as opening a 'Pandora's Box'.

69 'He Jiankui', *Wikipedia*, https://en.wikipedia.org/wiki/He_Jiankui (retrieved 7 April 2021).

70 Dennis Normile, 'Chinese Scientist Who Produced Genetically Altered Babies Sentenced to 3 Years in Jail', *Science*, 30 December 2019, www.sciencemag.org/news/2019/12/chinese-scientist-who-produced-genetically-altered-babies-sentenced-3-years-jail (retrieved 7 April 2021). The resulting twin girls are at time of writing apparently healthy and normal, and safe from HIV infection.

71 Jennifer Doudna, 'How CRISPR Lets Us Edit Our DNA', TED Talk, www.ted.com/talks/jennifer_doudna_how_crispr_lets_us_edit_our_dna/up-next?language=en (retrieved 7 April 2021).

72 Today's descendants of Dr Johnson's Jamaican servant Francis Barber, he and his successors all having had white English spouses, show no traces of their Jamaican heritage after four generations over two-and-a-half centuries; two millennia of segregation might be expected to preserve or

create more marked differences. 'First Encounters', *Black and British: A Forgotten History*, episode 1, 9 November 2016. BBC Television.

73 Jonathan Glover, *What Sort of People Should There Be?* (London: Pelican, 1984). This is the first study of the ethics of genetics and psychoneurology. Writing of this excellent book many years after it had gone out of print, Glover said, 'This book is about some questions to do with the future of mankind. The questions have been selected on two grounds. They arise out of scientific developments whose beginnings we can already see, such as genetic engineering and behaviour control. And they involve fundamental values: these technologies may change the central framework of human life'; www.jonathanglover.org/books/what-sort-of-people-should-there-be (retrieved 7 April 2021).

74 The insurance example is non-trivial: if you can't get driver's insurance you can't take employment where driving is essential; if your house is burgled you cannot restore material losses; if you can't get travel insurance you may be liable for extreme costs in an emergency, or forbidden to travel to some places altogether.

75 In this section of the discussion I make use of points raised in Grayling, *Democracy and Its Crisis*, and also *The Good State*.

76 'Russian Agents Were Behind Yahoo Hack, US Says', *New York Times*, 15 March 2017, www.nytimes.com/2017/03/15/technology/yahoo-hack-indictment.html (retrieved 7 April 2021).

77 *First Draft*, https://firstdraftnews.org (retrieved 7 April 2021).

78 'The Guardian View on Big Data: The Danger is Less Democracy', *Guardian*, 26 February 2017, www.theguardian.com/commentisfree/2017/feb/26/the-guardian-view-on-big-data-the-danger-is-less-democracy (retrieved 7 April 2021).

79 Ibid.

80 Daniel Kahneman, *Thinking, Fast and Slow* (London: Penguin, 2013).

81 See Grayling, *Democracy and Its Crisis* (2017) for an account of how representative democracy was devised to honour the two but not automatically connected rights at issue: the right of the people to be the final political authority in the state, and the right of the people to have 'good enough' government to serve their interests.

3 Justice and Rights

1 Max Roser and Esteban Ortiz-Ospina, 'Global Extreme Poverty', *Our World in Data*, https://ourworldindata.org/extreme-poverty (retrieved

18 June 2021). The figures are calculated on adjusted purchasing power.

2 UNDP, 'The 2020 Global Multidimensional Poverty Index (MPI)', http://hdr.undp.org/en/2020-MPI (retrieved 18 June 2021).

3 The criteria are listed in ibid.

4 UN, 'The 17 Goals', https://sdgs.un.org/goals (retrieved 18 June 2021).

5 William Shakespeare, *King Lear*, Act 3, Scene 4, ll. 28–36.

6 In conversation with the author in the Green Room of a Sydney radio station, Muhammad Yunus said that his new mission was to persuade young people not to look for work after finishing their education, but to start their own enterprises.

7 Dominic Frisby, 'Wealth Inequality Is Soaring – Here Are the 10 Reasons Why It's Happening', *Guardian*, 12 April 2018, www.theguardian.com/commentisfree/2018/apr/12/wealth-inequality-reasons-richest-global-gap (retrieved 9 April 2021).

8 Reaz Haider, 'Climate Change-Induced Salinity Affecting Soil across Coastal Bangladesh', *Reliefweb*, 15 January 2019, https://reliefweb.int/report/bangladesh/climate-change-induced-salinity-affecting-soil-across-coastal-bangladesh (retrieved 9 April 2021).

9 Peter Singer, *The Most Good You Can Do* (New Haven: Yale University Press, 2015). My friend and colleague Peter Singer has provided the most eloquent and persuasive – in fact unanswerable – single account of what an individual can do, from the comfort of a good standard of living in a developed country, and without being much discommoded, to contribute to the reduction of world poverty.

10 'Poverty 101: How Can We End Global Poverty Once and for All?', *The Correspondent*, https://thecorrespondent.com/10181/poverty-101-how-can-we-end-global-poverty-once-and-for-all/443596351-243043df (retrieved 9 April 2021).

11 The United Nations' Sustainable Development Goals, www.un.org (retrieved 9 April 2021).

12 Rebecca Lake, 'The Hidden Penalty of Motherhood', *The Balance*, 3 March 2021, www.thebalance.com/how-the-hidden-penalty-of-motherhood-affects-women-careers-4164215 (retrieved 10 April 2021).

13 Robert Garland, *The Greek Way of Life* (Ithaca: Cornell University Press, 1990), p. 18.

14 John Studd, 'A Comparison of 19th Century and Contemporary Attitudes to Female Sexuality', *Gynecological Endocrinology*, 23 (2007), pp. 673–81, https://pubmed.ncbi.nlm.nih.gov/18075842/ (retrieved 10 April 2021).

15 John Studd, 'Ovariotomy for Menstrual Madness and Premenstrual

Syndrome – 19th Century History and Lessons for Current Practice', *Gynecological Endocrinology*, 22 (2006), www.tandfonline.com/doi/full /10.1080/09513590600881503 (retrieved 10 April 2021). See also Sarah W. Rodriguez, 'Rethinking the History of Female Circumcision and Clitoridectomy', *Journal of the History of Medicine and Allied Sciences*, 63 (2008), pp. 323–47.

16 Garland, *The Greek Way of Life*, p. 244.

17 Cecilia Tasca, Mariangela Rapetti, Mauro Giovanni Carta, and Bianca Fadda, 'Women and Hysteria in the History of Mental Health', *Clinical Practice and Epidemiology in Mental Health*, 8 (2012), pp. 110–19.

18 Ibid., p. 114.

19 Susan B. Sorenson, 'Gender Disparities in Injury Mortality: Consistent, Persistent, and Larger Than You'd Think', *American Journal of Public Health*, 101 (2011), www.ncbi.nlm.nih.gov/pmc/articles/PMC3222499 (retrieved 11 April 2021).

20 WHO, 'Violence Against Women', 9 March 2021, www.who.int/news-room /fact-sheets/detail/violence-against-women (retrieved 10 April 2021).

21 UN, 'The World's Women 2020: Trends and Statistics', 20 October 2020, www.un.org/en/desa/world's-women-2020 (retrieved 10 April 2021).

22 See Helen Pankhurst, *Deeds Not Words* (London: Sceptre, 2018).

23 I recount the following in more detail in A. C. Grayling, *Towards the Light* (London: Bloomsbury, 2007), and draw on that account here. Reprising the story is important as a contribution to continuing the gender equality effort, given how far from complete it is.

24 Quoted in Grayling, *Towards the Light*, chapter 5.

25 Mary Wollstonecraft, *A Vindication of the Rights of Woman* (London: Penguin Classics, rev. ed., 2004).

26 Ibid., Dedicatory Epistle.

27 The label 'second wave feminism' was coined by the journalist Martha Lear in an article in the *New York Times Magazine*, March 1968.

28 When the National Organization of Women (NOW) was founded in 1966 its 'Statement of Purpose' said that women's right to equality was part of the nationwide demand for general civil rights.

29 Kristin Rowe-Finkbeiner, *The F Word: Feminism in Jeopardy* (Emeryville, CA: Seal Press, 2004).

30 Elizabeth Evans, *The Politics of Third Wave Feminisms: Neoliberalism, Intersectionality, and the State in Britain and the US* (London: Palgrave Macmillan, 2015).

31 Jacquetta A. Newman and Linda Ann White, *Women, Politics, and Public Policy*, 2nd ed. (Toronto: Oxford University Press, 2012).

32 Quoted in Grayling, *War*, pp. 208–9.
33 Quoted in ibid., p. 209.
34 Quoted in ibid., p. 210.
35 Quoted in ibid., p. 211.
36 'The Countries Where Homosexuality Is Illegal', *The Week*, 3 April 2020, www.theweek.co.uk/96298/the-countries-where-homosexuality-is-still-illegal (retrieved 21 April 2021).
37 Alia Chughtai, 'Know Their Names: Black People Killed by the Police in the US', *Al-Jazeera*, https://interactive.aljazeera.com/aje/2020/know-their-names/index.html (retrieved 21 April 2021).
38 Elections for the US House of Representatives and the UK's House of Commons are conducted on the plurality – 'first-past-the-post' – system, which results in election of representatives on a minority of votes cast in cases where three or more candidates stand, splitting the vote among them. See Grayling, *Democracy and Its Crisis*, pp. 138–42, and *The Good State*, pp. 18–19 and 168–9.
39 A lack of paper qualifications is by no means an invariable guide to intellectual capacity or potential.
40 John Rawls, *A Theory of Justice* (Cambridge, MA: Belknap Press, revised edition, 1999), p. 261.
41 Ibid.
42 Ibid.
43 Robert Nozick, *Anarchy, State, and Utopia* (New York: Basic Books, 1974).
44 Jeremy Bentham, *Anarchical Fallacies*, in John Bowring (ed.), *The Works of Jeremy Bentham*, Vol. 2 (Edinburgh: William Tate, 1838–43).
45 Some scholars locate the origin of the concept of rights in Grotius and Pufendorf in the seventeenth century, some as early as Gratian in the twelfth century, or in the debate about Franciscan poverty; yet others see the concept present in substance and implication very much earlier still, in Aristotle, Cicero, and elsewhere.
46 For Locke the origin of property lies in people 'mixing their labour' with what they find in nature. John Locke, *Second Treatise of Government* (1689).
47 Implicit in this argument is a repudiation of the 'is–ought' distinction in ethics, this being the claim that one cannot deduce a *prescription*, a statement of obligation of the form 'you ought to do so-and-so', from a *description* of how things contingently are. The claim that the concept of rights lies in the experience of wrongs is the claim that the justifications we offer for our ethical prescriptions is drawn from knowledge – hence,

descriptions – of what can respectively obstruct and promote the basics of human flourishing.

48 In 1997, some months before the return of Hong Kong to Chinese sovereignty, I ran a conference, based at Hong Kong University, on the question of the universality of human rights. The PRC sent a delegation to argue the anti-universalist case. At that time, working with an NGO at the Human Rights Commission in Geneva on serious human rights violations in China, I was very familiar with the PRC's advocates in this cause; they had a large and skilful team present in Geneva to protect the PRC's reputation and to ensure that enough support was garnered among nations represented there to block votes of censure against it.

4 Relativism

1 'Department of Justice Interface Programme – Department of Justice', *Justice*, 31 July 2017, www.justice-ni.gov.uk/articles/department-justice-interface-programme (retrieved 18 June 2021).

2 More precisely, between the conquest of Spain by the Ummayyads in the early eighth century to the expulsion in 1492 of the Jews by the 'Catholic monarchs' Isabella I of Castile and Ferdinand II of Aragon whose marriage unified Spain.

3 See Grayling, *The Age of Genius* (London: Bloomsbury, 2017) and *Descartes: The Life and Times of a Genius* (London: Free Press, 2005).

4 Ibid., pp. 63–4.

5 J. Kelly, 'Is Football Bigotry Confined to the West of Scotland? The Heart of Midlothian and Hibernian Rivalry', in J. Flint and J. Kelly (eds), *Bigotry, Football and Scotland* (Edinburgh: Edinburgh University Press, 2013), www.pure.ed.ac.uk/ws/portalfiles/portal/15242619/Is_football_bigotry_confined_to_the_west_of_Scotland.pdf (retrieved 14 April 2021).

6 I do this in my *Refutation of Scepticism* (Aurora, IL: Open Court, 1985), an early effort to show that sceptical challenges to the veridicality of perceptual experience can be overcome on Kantian grounds by appealing to fundamental features of conceptual cognitive architecture – a categorial approach for which a deduction can be given. For those familiar with similar approaches in epistemology, the idea makes use of Donald Davidson's view that nothing can count as a conceptual scheme unless it is accessible (if a conceptual scheme is represented as a language then *translatability* is the criterion of its existence), from which it follows that there can only be one; and therefore cognitive relativism fails.

7 FGM is a practice that appears to have arisen in Africa in a wide region from Somalia to Nigeria, and to have become associated with certain forms of Islam (for a particular example Shaif'i Sunni Islam). There are certain 'weak' (*da'if*) hadith attributed to Muhammad describing the practice as 'noble', but the Al-Azhar Supreme Council of Research at the mosque of that name in Cairo ruled in 2007 that the practice has no place in 'core Islamic law or partial provisions'. This statement was reported by UNICEF on 2 July 2007. One notes that the campaign to end FGM in Islam continues. 'Female Genital Cutting and Islam', *Orchid Project*, 11 March 2015, www.orchidproject.org/female-genital-cutting-and-islam/?gclid=Cj0KCQjwpdqDBhCSARIsAEUJ0hMXcfG6NQB7CuOKE7Jc C2H3nnFB7RBGINzCkHq_M1aJveemGtZQ5csaAjxEEALw_wcB (retrieved 14 April 2021).

5 The Solution

1 One should look at history: injustice and poverty have caused hundreds of uprisings and revolutions just in the modern period in Europe alone. It is foolish to imagine that they will not happen again, not least as the combination of pressures – poverty, climate-change difficulties, the availability of medical and other kinds of help restricted to those who can pay – increases desperation and anger. The world stands at present on the edges of several cliffs at once.

2 'Extinction Rebellion' – which I support; as with almost everything in the world, hope lies with the young – has alas had this effect in some quarters. Its work requires the adjunct of sustained public education so that its activism can spark a wider public activism to force the pace on climate solutions. See https://extinctionrebellion.uk

3 This is a proposal made in 2021 by Finland's president Sauli Niinistö.

4 On the nature of genuine and effective democracy, see Grayling, *The Good State* (2020).

5 I am proud to be involved in supporting Rogbonko School in Sierra Leone, an initiative of Aminatta Forna in which I became involved at its inception; Aminatta Forna, 'The Rogbonko Village Project in Sierra Leone', https://aminattaforna.com/rogbonko.html (retrieved 18 June 2021).

6 See Grayling, *The Good State* (2020) for an examination of the conditions of genuine democracy. I draw on that discussion here; the themes of that discussion are inextricably entwined with the discussion here.

7 Ibid., pp. 147–8, 168–9.
8 On Russia, see Garry Kasparov, 'Russian Democracy Is a Farce. Putin Wants the Same Fate for America', *CNN*, 5 July 2020, https://edition. cnn.com/2020/07/05/opinions/russian-democracy-is-a-farce-kasparov/index.html (retrieved 18 June 2021).
9 See Grayling, *The Good State*, 'Conclusion', pp. 165 et seq.
10 See 'Freedom of Expression', in A. C. Grayling, *Ideas That Matter* (London: Weidenfeld & Nicolson, 2009).
11 To short-circuit what is sometimes called the 'no true Scotsman' fallacy, note that I have given an express account of what a 'genuine' democracy would be: representative, constitutionally controlled, shaped towards government by multi-party agreement.
12 A declaration of interest: as a Patron of *Dignity in Dying* in the UK and a member of *Dignitas* should its services be required, I regard the right to physician-assisted suicide as an entailment of the right to life. In several right-to-die cases in the courts I have submitted *amicus curiae* briefs on the subject, arguing in essence that this follows from rights considerations relating to the quality of life, individual autonomy, and the availability of medical means to provide a calm and painless exit from an unwanted existence – all under the proviso that it is the subject's own settled and rational wish for this; no third party can take such a decision for anyone else other than those in long-term vegetative states.

INDEX

223